GHOSTS
OF THE
BERKSHIRES

GHOSTS
OF THE
BERKSHIRES

ROBERT OAKES

Haunted
America

Published by Haunted America
A Division of The History Press
Charleston, SC
www.historypress.com

First published 2020

Manufactured in the United States

ISBN 9781467142793

Library of Congress Control Number: 2020938584

Notice: The information in this book is true and complete to the best of our knowledge. It is offered without guarantee on the part of the author or The History Press. The author and The History Press disclaim all liability in connection with the use of this book.

CONTENTS

CONTENTS

ACKNOWLEDGEMENTS

For your support and contributions, I want to thank: Nini Gilder; John Demos; Joe Durwin; Sam Baltrusis; Jeff Belanger; everyone at the Mount, especially Anne Schuyler, Marge Cox, Elric Walker, Patricia Pin and Susan Wissler; Will Boyce; Tim Marvin; Grace and Jason Knopp; the Lee Library; Margaret Morrissey; Sonia Morrison at the Otis Historical Commission; Barbara Greenbaum; Gabriel Kosakoff; Bernadette Horgan; Erin Asbury; Bridget Carr; Bill Cosel; Linda Rocke; Mike Kinsella; Holly Ketron; Tina Packer; Cindy Dickinson; Jessy McMahon; Ruth Burday; the Murphy family; Jeannie Maschino; Matt Tannenbaum; my professors and fellow students at Bread Loaf; Dick and Dorothy Robson; Kim Ostellino; Heather Anello; Richard Greene; Abbey Keith; Lee Mullins; the Chain Gang; T.W. Collins; Kate Barton; my students and their families; the Nickerson family; the Smith family; my family; my wife, Katherine; and the ghosts of the Berkshires.

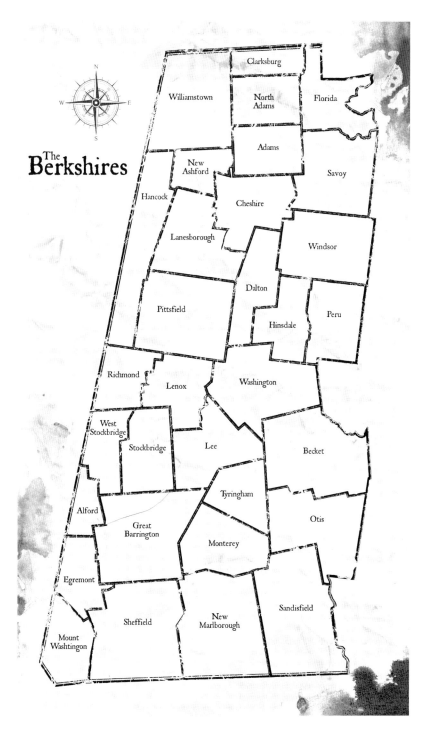

The Berkshires

Clarksburg

Williamstown

North Adams

Florida

Adams

New Ashford

Savoy

Hancock

Cheshire

Lanesborough

Windsor

Dalton

Pittsfield

Peru

Hinsdale

Richmond

Lenox

Washington

West Stockbridge

Stockbridge

Lee

Becket

Alford

Tyringham

Great Barrington

Otis

Monterey

Egremont

Mount Washtingon

Sheffield

New Marlborough

Sandisfield

Courtesy of Robert Oakes.

INTRODUCTION

There is something lurking in the shadows of the Berkshires. Ghost seekers, for instance, often feel uneasy on the second floor of the stable at Edith Wharton's the Mount. It is cluttered and dusty and smells of old wood. And on windy nights, they can hear thumps and bumps and creaking boards. Moving through this space, as their flashlights push the shadows back, they sometimes see what looks like movement in the dark beyond the beams. As a ghost tour guide, I tell groups about what others have seen here: a hanged woman, a crouching figure with piercing eyes, a disembodied head in the hallway. Together, we peer into the darkness and wonder: What are we about to see?

While researching for this book, I asked myself that question many times. And at each location I explored, I found the palpable presence of such entities, as evidenced by the sheer number of stories that have been told about them for years. The Berkshires has been a haunted region since its earliest days, when it was a rugged, sparsely populated frontier. As the Mohicans, European fur traders and early settlers walked the old-growth forests on narrow footpaths through branches and brambles, they must have felt both fear and awe. They must have sensed the spirits with them everywhere they turned. And through the years of revolutionary fervor and industrial enterprise, through the splendor of the Gilded Age and the tourism of today, sensations like these have inspired many tales of shadowy figures, voices of spirits, spectral trains and a ghostly girl in a forgotten cemetery. These haunted Berkshires lie just beneath the region's bucolic beauty, a hidden world brought to light by the storytellers who share our ghostly lore.

Since 2010, I have told tales like these at the Mount and have asked visitors to venture with me into the unknown, opening themselves up to the possibility that they, too, might encounter something strange. Whether or not we actually see or hear anything, I believe the experience is worthwhile because, whenever we reach out, with our senses open and our imagination engaged, we do make contact with the presence that so many have felt here over the years. It awakens us to the profound mysteries that lie beneath the world we know. So, journey with me through these haunted Berkshires as I share with you some of the many eerie tales I have uncovered. Let's reach out together, into the darkness, and discover what mysteries may lie beyond the beam of our flashlight.

1.
GHOSTS IN THE HILLS

WIZARD'S GLEN

While driving along Gulf Road in Dalton, passing the last of the houses near the intersection of Park and High Streets, you might find yourself drawn toward the place where the neighborhood disappears into the woods. There, the pavement ends, and the road becomes a twisted track of dirt and stone. Ominously, an orange sign beside the road warns: "Use at your own risk." Passing the sign, you feel a change in the atmosphere; the air becomes cooler, and the light dims. And as you proceed, the forest entangles and surrounds you. From there, Gulf Road winds its way through the trees, threading through a towering glen of huge, tumbled stones before connecting on the other side with Route 8, near the Berkshire Mall.

More than a century ago, local residents called this glen the Gulf, and according to Joseph E.A. Smith, who wrote about the location in his 1852 book *Taghconic, Or, Letters and Legends About Our Summer Home*, it was considered a bucolic place to "pass a merry hour…in the cool depths of the ravine," perhaps while enjoying a good book or a picnic lunch. But early settlers seemed to feel a sense of dread about the place. They called it Wizard's Glen, a name that reflected the commonly held belief that Native American shamans, whom they called wizards, used the location to perform rituals that were little understood and greatly feared. In his 1896 book, *Myths and Legends of Our Own Land*, Charles M. Skinner described the scene this way:

A twisted track of dirt and stone, Gulf Road winds its way through Wizard's Glen. *Courtesy of Robert Oakes.*

"Here, the Indian priests performed their incantations, and on the red-stained Devil's Altar, it was said they offered human sacrifice to Hobomocko and his demons of the wood." The "Devil's Altar" refers to a large flat rock that still prominently juts out from the hillside. Its red stains are now thought to be iron ore deposits in the stone, but it is easy to see why superstitious settlers would have viewed these blood-red blots as evidence of grisly human sacrifice, suspicious as they were of the native people and their ways.

This suspicion is reflected in Skinner's demonic description of Hobomocko, a spirit of the underworld the Native Americans often prayed to in musical incantations at sacred sites like this. With its mass of stones, which are scattered in heaps on the steep hillside in such a way as to create numerous openings into darkness below, the Glen must have seemed an ideal place of passage into the spirit realm, or, as in the case of a priest known as Tashmu, who is mentioned in another of Skinner's tales, it seemed to serve as a place of oracle, where natives could learn the divine will. But to the early settlers, who saw Hobomocko as the Devil of scripture, or "the spirit of evil," the rituals conducted there could only be seen as satanic. So, it is not surprising that Wizard's Glen soon became known among the local townspeople as a place to avoid. It is also not surprising that one especially eerie tale about the Glen soon took root and began to grow.

It is the story of a man named John Chamberlain, a resident of Dalton who was returning at dusk from a day of hunting with a massive buck slung over his shoulder. Ignoring all warnings, Chamberlain decided to pass through the Glen, hoping to shorten his journey and arrive home before nightfall. But as he neared the Devil's Altar, a sudden storm broke the calm, pitching rain, wind, thunder and lightning through the swaying trees overhead. Left with no choice, Chamberlain scurried beneath a rocky outcropping beside the road, where he waited for the storm to pass, but it only grew worse.

As he lay with his head on the cold, stony ground, he saw a horrible sight. Not far ahead, along the path, the woods began to bend and twist, and through an unseen opening, hundreds of hideous creatures stepped out, carrying torches that burned with a pale blue light. There were demons with cloven feet, fiends with wings, vampires, imps and the spirits of the dead. Chamberlain gasped at the grotesque faces that were glistening with rainwater. His heart stopped as they passed mere feet from where he lay. From there, they tramped into the undergrowth and encircled the Devil's Altar. A sudden hush fell. Then, from the unseen opening, there came an immense figure with horns and a long, spiked tail. Chamberlain barely stifled a shriek as he set his eyes on the Devil himself. Then, another figure appeared; a native priest was gesturing wildly with his arms raised as he danced on the reddened stone.

At his command, the convocation began to chant hideously as several creatures dragged a terrified young woman out from the shadows. She was splayed out, shrieking on the bloodstained rock and tied down by her hands and feet. Then, the horde moved closer, clearly meaning to devour her. She let out a scream of such terror that Chamberlain was jolted into action. He knew that if he did nothing, he would be doomed to hear that horrible scream echo in his ears for the rest of his life, reminding him that he had let that poor woman die a gruesome death. So, reaching for the Bible tucked away in his pocket, he burst from the cave shouting out the Lord's Prayer. At this, the hideous creatures recoiled, the torches went out, the storm stopped suddenly and the entire hellish assembly vanished, leaving Chamberlain alone in the dark. Exhausted, he lay down under the stone outcrop, where he fell asleep. In the morning, when he woke, Chamberlain found nothing to prove the spectacle had been anything more than a dream—except that the body of the buck was gone.

The terrified woman was splayed out, shrieking on the bloodstained rock. *Courtesy of Katherine Oakes.*

It is certainly a dramatic story, though one that contains the troubling association of indigenous beliefs with evil spirits. Clearly, much of what we call monstrous depends on our own points of view. Still, the story continues to be told to this day. And the Glen continues to draw visitors. Some have marked the stones with spray paint, and several of the openings underneath—those imagined passages to the spirit realm—are now cluttered with beer cans and car batteries, the debris of the civilized. But if you stand quietly on those rocks, you may feel an ancient resonance, an echo of some mysterious power that has stirred the soul and inspired the imagination for generations. Maybe no one—not the native people, the early settlers, the nineteenth-century picnickers nor the modern-day spray painters—fully understands what it is, but surely there is something in the Glen that pulls us out of our familiar neighborhoods, past all warning signs and into the unknown.

THE HOOSAC TUNNEL

In the northernmost part of the county, near the city of North Adams, there is an opening in the side of a mountain through which several freight trains pass every day. Once inside, these trains must travel nearly five miles in total darkness beneath countless tons of heavy rock before emerging again into the light. Most conductors must think little of it; it's just another stretch of track to pass before their job is done. But some may find it hard to forget the stories—the tales of gruesome deaths, disembodied voices and eerie apparitions—that have been told for many years about the Hoosac Tunnel. These stories continue to capture the imagination and attract ghost seekers down those tracks and through the opening, like heroes on a journey to the underworld.

Standing on that threshold and peering in, you can see only the absence of light, a total void. When walking through, it is as if you are passing out of the world of the living and into a city of the dead. The cold, tomb-like atmosphere surrounds you. The neatly cut blocks overhead give way to pocked stone that looks as if something very old and very big has been

Peering into the Hoosac Tunnel, you can see only the absence of light. It's a total void. *Courtesy of Katherine Oakes.*

clawing away at it for many years, slowly gnawing its way out of the deep. It seems unnatural to go into the ground like this; everything inside you begs to return to the light. But if you were one of the miners who built the Hoosac Tunnel more than a century ago, you would have had to fight against this natural instinct every day. You would have had to delve deeper and deeper down into the dark, feeling as though you were being buried alive—as many were.

The Hoosac Tunnel Project was started in 1851 as a bold attempt to conquer an overwhelming natural obstacle: the Hoosac Range in the northern Berkshires. A spur of the Appalachians, some of the oldest mountains on Earth, these impenetrable heights effectively cut New Englanders off from the rest of the nation. Their solution to this isolation was to bore a nearly five-mile-long hole through Hoosac Mountain—from the town of Florida to the city of North Adams—allowing the railway line direct access to New York State and the western frontier beyond. By the time it was completed in 1875, the Hoosac Tunnel was hailed as an engineering marvel, one of the greatest achievements of the nineteenth century. But because so many men died during its construction, it also came to be known as the "Bloody Pit" and the "Tunnel from Hell," a cursed and haunted place that was feared by many.

The wretched nature and sheer danger of the work required to build the tunnel certainly did not help the project's reputation. To pierce a hole through the mountain meant the excavation of two million tons of rock, a grim and daunting task, especially given the technology that was available at the time. The workmen's first solution was to use a state-of-the-art tunnel-boring machine, which failed after the first ten feet. Undaunted, the workmen persisted, gnawing inch by inch into the ancient stone with a pneumatic drill, gunpowder, pickaxes and shovels. In 1865, progress was accelerated with the introduction of nitroglycerin, but because it was an extremely unstable explosive, it brought new dangers and led to the first widely reported disaster at the site. On March 20, 1865, explosive experts Ringo Kelley, Ned Brinkman and Billy Nash set a charge and ran for cover, though only Kelley made it back to the bunker alive. It seems he ignited the charge prematurely, burying the others beneath a ton of fallen rock. Kelley was not seen again until one year later, when he was found strangled to death at the very spot where the explosion had occurred. No one was ever charged with the crime, though many workers believed it was the angry ghosts of Brinkman and Nash who had taken revenge on Kelley that night.

Shortly after this incident occurred, many men began to report hearing the sound of disembodied voices and cries of agony coming from deep inside the rock. Many refused to enter the tunnel after sunset, and still, others walked off the project completely, slowing the pace of progress to a crawl. Though officials insisted the sound was that of wind howling through the tunnel, the men were not satisfied. So, investigators were brought in to search the tunnel in an attempt to calm the workmen's fears. This plan backfired, though, as the investigators themselves reported hearing the unsettling sound of groans in the deep, cold dark, which they believed were not caused by wind.

Possibly the most horrifying incident to occur at the site took place on October 17, 1867, when a crew of workmen descended into the central shaft. This massive hole, which was dug at the midpoint of the tunnel, allowed workers to burrow out from the center and join with the crews digging in from the east and west sides of the mountain. The shaft included an elevator with a hoist at the top; it was used to haul the heavy rock up from the hole. There were also pumps that kept it free of water and a one-thousand-foot vertical exhaust shaft that allowed for the ventilation of poisonous gasses. That day, while the crew was excavating the exhaust shaft, a candle in the hoist housing ignited naphtha fumes, setting off an explosion. The hoist collapsed into the shaft, raining fiery debris and freshly sharpened drill bits down onto the heads of the workmen below. And because the pumps were also destroyed, the shaft began to fill with water and noxious fumes.

A man who was sent down to attempt a rescue had to be pulled up quickly from the poisonous cloud. Once he was out, he reportedly gasped, "No hope," before slipping into unconsciousness. Officials concluded that the men below were beyond rescue, and no further attempts were made. Months later, workers did reach the bottom, only to discover that several of the men had survived the explosion and falling debris, living long enough to build a raft with which they attempted to float themselves to the surface before dying of suffocation. For nearly a year afterward, many workers and local residents claimed they saw apparitions of the lost miners moving through the mist and trees, toward the shaft, with tools slung over their shoulders. It was said that the apparitions would vanish suddenly, leaving no trace in the snow on the mountaintop. Others said they could hear the faint sound of cries emanating from the earth below their feet. These eerie reports persisted until the last of the thirteen bodies was recovered and laid to rest.

In spite of the many disasters and delays, the tunnel project was, at last, completed, though at a higher cost in both time and money than anyone had anticipated. But it was the human cost that cut the deepest. In all, nearly two hundred of the project's roughly eight hundred workmen died, mostly in explosions and collapses. Tales of their ordeals and gruesome deaths and reports of lingering spirits in the dark have continued to haunt the surrounding hills ever since, attracting ghost seekers who report bizarre experiences of their own. One local hunter claimed to hear "strange voices" that lured him into the opening, where he said he was accosted by entities that left him battered and beaten. Others claim to have seen odd lights, orbs and phantom figures, and they claim to have heard the sounds of muffled voices and heavy wet footsteps along the rails. Some especially bold adventurers have even dared to walk the entire five miles of the tunnel, from end to end. Several claimed to feel as if something unseen walked behind or beside them. But it is certainly not advisable to walk the length of the tunnel. Several trains still pass through every day, and that light you see coming toward you on the tracks may not be a ghostly miner after all.

The Old Coot of Mount Greylock

There is something about mountains that inspires the imagination. Towering high above the surrounding landscape, mountains lift up our eyes, our thoughts and our spirits, and they give us a reason to dream. Mount Greylock, the highest point in Massachusetts, has long inspired the imagination of many in the Berkshires and beyond. As he wrote *Moby Dick*, Herman Melville famously looked out through the window of his study at Arrowhead in Pittsfield and saw in the distant peaks of Greylock a surfacing great white whale. Joseph E.A. Smith (also known as Godfrey Greylock), in *Taghconic, Or, Letters and Legends About Our Summer Home*, remarked how easy it was to imagine supernatural creatures along the slopes of the mountain. "Some of the openings in the woods almost persuade one that the days of fairy gambols are not yet past [and]…in these…very rings of fresh green grass…the elfin revels must still be nightly held." And more recently, J.K. Rowling envisioned a school of wizardry at the top of Mount Greylock, hidden behind a wreath of clouds.

Wreaths of clouds often surround the summit of Mount Greylock, reducing the usual view of ninety miles in all directions on a clear day to a few foggy feet. If you were to visit the mountaintop under such conditions, you could take shelter from the fog at the rustic stone and timber Bascom Lodge. You could sit beside a roaring fire and listen to the wind blow against the rocks

At the top of Mount Greylock, the rustic Bascom Lodge offers shelter from the fog. *Courtesy of T.W. Collins.*

and trees outside. On such a night, you might also hear a storyteller, like park interpreter Michael Whalen, share lore inspired by this dark and moody mountain. The most famous of all is the tale of the Old Coot, the spirit of a Civil War veteran who is said to haunt the woods near the intersection of the Bellows Pipe and Thunderbolt Trails.

According to the story, before he became known as the Old Coot, William Saunders was a young husband, father and farmer who owned a parcel of land along the lower slopes of the mountain, near the town of North Adams. When the Civil War broke out, Saunders, like so many young men at the time, left his wife and children to tend the farm alone and marched off to war, not knowing if he would ever return. Saunders was badly injured and nearly died, but he did manage to survive the war, driven on by the hope of returning home. Sadly, his wife, Belle, only heard that her husband had been gravely injured, and as weeks turned into months and no further word came, Belle assumed the worst. She waited as long as she could, but eventually, she took a new husband, a man named Milton Cliffords, whom Saunders had hired to work the farm in his absence. Cliffords cared for Belle and looked after the children as if they were his own. Time passed, the farm prospered and the newly mended family moved on.

One day, long after the war's end, a grizzled man in a worn-out Union uniform arrived in town. He was a native son, though no one recognized him, as the war had changed Bill Saunders. He had grown thin and pale and looked much older than his years. Still nursing his wounds, Saunders shambled up to his old farm and leaned against the gate to look in. He saw his children run to another man and call him "Daddy"; he watched his wife embrace her new husband. He saw life on the farm continuing without him. Not wanting to destroy their happiness, Saunders decided, right then and there, never to reveal himself. With a small savings of his wartime wages, he purchased a piece of land farther up the mountain and built himself a tiny one-room cabin.

During the summer months, Saunders took work as a day laborer on area farms, including, on occasion, his own, but no one recognized him, not even his wife and children. Townsfolk only knew him as the strange "Old Coot" who lived all alone in the woods up on the mountain; he was often seen wandering near the Bellows Pipe Trail. Out there, in the ramshackle cabin, Saunders passed the winter months beside his woodstove, keeping warm and waiting for spring. But during one especially cold night in late January, a blast of wind blew open his door, snuffing out the fire. Saunders never lived to see another spring, for he froze to death in his sleep that night. Some days later, as the story goes, a group of hunters came upon the cabin and discovered Saunders's frozen, lifeless body within it. When they opened the door, they were startled to see a shadowy figure rise up and pass through the wall, disappearing into the twilit woods beyond. Before running off to tell the authorities, the hunters found documents inside that positively identified the frozen man as poor old Bill, who had lived among them all along.

Ever since that day, many say the ghost of the Old Coot still lingers near the intersection of the Bellows Pipe and Thunderbolt Trails, especially during the last two weeks of January. The story of the Old Coot first appeared in print on January 19, 1939, in an article published in the *North Adams Transcript* alongside a piece promoting the upcoming Thunderbolt downhill ski race. The article advised readers to be on the lookout for the Coot, who, if not frightened away by the crowds, could be seen "in the late afternoon, near the bend before the final dip of the ski run." Such exact details concerning the time and place of the expected appearance have led some to conclude that the entire tale was nothing more than a publicity stunt cooked up to help promote the race; others wonder whether the story contained some historical truth.

Whether or not it has any basis in actual fact, the legend of the Old Coot certainly has had staying power. One week after that first mention in the *Transcript*, another article about the Coot appeared; this time, it was accompanied by a photograph taken by *Transcript* photographer P. Randolph Trabold that allegedly captured the image of Saunders himself. According to the report, Trabold and a group of "ghost raisers" ventured into the wild on the hunt for the Coot. They survived three nights in the wintry woods before finally encountering the ghost. The grainy image shows a hunched and emaciated figure lurching toward the tree line, with one hand exposed and its head turned away from the camera's eye. A reference to this photograph appeared again in the *Transcript* in 1965, followed up by yet another photograph of the elusive Coot in the 1970s. Many locals have claimed to have spotted the mysterious figure or to have heard the stories. Legend hunters and ghostwriters have all noted the persistence of the tale. As recently as 2005, an event listing in the *Berkshire Eagle* promoted a "search [of the] lower Thunderbolt area for signs of Old Coot."

Regardless of its authenticity, the tale of the Old Coot, like the mountain he is said to haunt, has captured the imagination of many in the Berkshires and beyond. And it should surprise no one if Saunders himself emerges from the Greylock fog one night to warm himself beside the fire at Bascom Lodge.

THE FORBIDDEN LOVERS OF PONTOOSUC LAKE

On a summer day, Pontoosuc Lake in Pittsfield and Lanesborough may be brimming with kayakers and motorboaters, swimmers and sunbathers, fishermen and dockside merrymakers. But as the sun sets and the moon rises, mist and silence settle on the water. It is during those twilight hours that many have claimed to notice strange shapes and haunting sounds float across the surface of the lake. In his 1879 book, *Taghconic: The Romance and Beauty of the Hills*, Pittsfield historian Joseph E.A. Smith alluded to a shadowy boat and boatman that are "often seen to flit over its midnight waters, as if in quest of that which it is doomed never to find." Smith described his own walks along the shoreline during the "witching hour…when the pale moon shed a very ghostly light upon the waters, while the shrieks, screams and howlings that hurtled, discordant upon the air, defied all my 'ologies to assign them to any known beast, bird or reptile." Though Smith admitted he

On Pontoosuc Lake at twilight, many have sensed the presence of something otherworldly. *Courtesy of Katherine Oakes.*

himself never "caught sight of this flitting ghostship," he described just the sort of mysterious atmosphere that has inspired many visitors of Pontoosuc Lake to sense the presence of something otherworldly.

The best-known Pontoosuc ghost story is that of Moon-keek and Shoon-keek, two young Mohicans whose tale of forbidden love may have been told in the days when their people lived along the lakeshore. According to some sources, in fact, the early Mohicans called the lake Shoon-keek-Moon-keek, possibly in reference to the legend. Though passionate and true, the love of Moon-keek and Shoon-keek was doomed from the start, as the laws of their tribe forbade the marriage of cousins. Moon-keek was the daughter of the tribal chief, and Shoon-keek was the son of the chief's brother. Though the chief was sympathetic, the law was quite clear on this point; he had no choice but to command the young lovers to keep apart. This, of course, they could not do; their feelings for one another were far too fierce.

Often, they met in secret in the woods or by the waterside, thinking they were free from prying eyes. But another young man, Nock-a-wan-do, was always following, always watchful, for he, too, wanted the beautiful Moon-keek. As Shoon-keek openly declared his love for her to the moon and stars above, the jealous Nock-a-wan-do slinked in the shadows, making his plans, biding his time. His time to act was close, for the forbidden lovers had formed a plan of their own; they were going to escape by boat and travel to a village beyond the far shore, where the law would not prohibit them from marrying. They were each going to paddle a canoe to an island in the lake, where they would meet and continue, side by side. They had vowed to stay together no matter what might happen. Should one of them not reach the island alive, the other would commit suicide so that they might be reunited in the afterlife.

Moon-keek was the first to reach the island. As she looked back over the water, she could see her lover paddling toward her. What she could not see was Nock-a-wan-do hiding in the shadows on the shore, and she could not see his arrow fly and pierce her dear one's heart. She did see his body slump and fall into the water, and she cried out, "Shoon-keek, Shoon-keek," as she paddled her canoe toward his. Then, suddenly, she stopped with a gasp. The phantom of her lover sat inside his boat, upright, arms folded, eyes set straight ahead, peering into the spirit world beyond. It slowly approached her, moved by an unseen hand, and as it passed her by, she could hear his voice calling to her, "Moon-keek, Moon-keek." Remembering her vow, Moon-keek stood and sang a mournful song; then, she threw herself into the lake and drowned. Just like her lover's, her canoe continued on across the water, piloted by the dead maiden's ghost. From the shadows on the shore, Nock-a-wan-do saw the two canoes floating side by side and heard the lovers' voices crying out from somewhere beyond the world, "Shoon-keek, Moon-keek, Shoon-keek, Moon-keek." When he returned to the village, Nock-a-wan-do was a shadow of himself. What he had witnessed on the lake that night stalked him for the rest of his life.

To this day, people say they hear the lovers' voices in the silence on Pontoosuc Lake. And some have claimed to have seen them paddling gently, side by side, making for some other shore where their love won't be forbidden.

The Spirit Voices of Bash Bish Falls

She stood in the moonlight, wrapped in a white linen robe. Below her was a deep drop of rushing water crashing and cascading on the boulders. It was June, the time of year when the moon crosses at just the right height to fill the shaggy ravine with a milky pale light. The man who stood below, gazing up at the granite outcrop that split the rushing water into twin falls, thought he saw her faintly in the mist. He thought he heard a voice coming from the water: "Follow me, my child." Looking down into the pool where the falling water foamed and crashed, he thought he saw a smiling face and felt strangely comforted. He felt all would be well if he went with her under the water. Looking back up toward the top of the falls, he was startled to find the phantom had locked eyes with his. "Join me," she said, with her arms outstretched. Then, she leapt and vanished.

Stories like this have been told of Bash Bish Falls, which is located in Mount Washington in the southwestern corner of the Berkshires, since at least the latter part of the nineteenth century. Inspired by the gloom of the deep gorge and the mesmerizing noise of rushing water, many visitors to these towering falls in the four-thousand-acre Mount Washington State Forest believe the place is alive with strange spirits in the mist and the sound of voices in the woods and water.

Local lore says that the Mohican tribes that once inhabited the area were also wary of the falls, believing them to be haunted by the spirit of a water witch they called Bash Bish. As the story goes, Bash Bish was a beautiful young woman who was much loved by all except for one jealous friend who began spreading rumors that she had been unfaithful to her husband. Though she insisted on her innocence, Bash Bish was found guilty by the tribal council and was sentenced to death by drowning. On the day she was to die, Bash Bish was brought to the top of the falls, where she was to be tied to a canoe and sent over. But to the amazement of onlookers, the young woman was suddenly surrounded by a halo of sunlight and butterflies. The tribesmen were afraid. Was this the presence of the Great Spirit or the dark powers of witchcraft? Seizing her opportunity in this moment of confusion, Bash Bish ran to the edge of the falls and threw herself over the edge. As she fell, they say the butterflies and sunlight enveloped her body, which was never found in the pool below. From that day on, the legend grew of the witch who lived within the falls. Some said they could see her form in the falling water. Many reported hearing an eerie voice above the crashing and splashing; it was repeatedly speaking her name or calling unwary travelers to her. All stayed as far away from the place as possible, fearing the witch's curse.

But the tale does not end there, for Bash Bish was said to have left behind an infant daughter, White Swan, who grew to become one of the most beautiful women in the village. And when the time came for Whirling Wind, the son of the chief, to take a wife, White Swan was chosen for him—but he was never told that she was the daughter of Bash Bish. At first, the marriage was happy; White Swan and Whirling Wind were in love. But when the young woman was unable to bear a child, a dark cloud settled over their marriage. It was imperative that Whirling Wind, who was next in line to lead the tribe, produce a male heir to continue the line of tribal chiefs. So, it was decided that he would take another wife who could bear him a son. White Swan bore this as best she could; she understood the need to continue the line, but the presence of this other woman tortured her.

Over time, White Swan grew pale and thin. She began to wander away from the village at night to linger by the forbidden falls, lured there by the mesmerizing voices in the water. One night, worried for his wife, Whirling Wind followed her to the falls, and he found her standing on the high rocks above, lit by the moon. He called to her, and she spoke—but not to him. She seemed to be answering a voice in the water below that only she could hear. "Mother, I am here. Take me." Whirling Wind then saw a white-robed figure reach toward her from the falls. In that moment, all became clear; he knew the secret that had been kept from him—his wife was the daughter of the water witch. Their marriage was cursed. He clambered up the rocks and reached to pull her from the edge, but she looked at him and leapt. Distraught, he leapt after her. In the morning, the search party found only the body of Whirling Wind broken on the rocks.

For years afterward, many said they saw the spirit of Bash Bish, seemingly at peace, happily reunited with White Swan. Some claimed to see her smiling face in the moonlit water; others said they spotted the forms of both mother and daughter in the twin falls. Many heard the sound of spirit voices in the water, eternally repeating the name of the witch: Bash Bish, Bash Bish, Bash Bish.

It may be that this tale has nothing at all to do with the Mohicans, who once inhabited this region. It is very likely it was an invention of the white folk who began to settle the area in the late 1600s—the Dutch farmers from New York and, later, the operators of the many iron forges that once stood nearby. Beginning in 1852, when the extension of the Harlem Line Railroad made the region accessible, travelers and tourists began to flock there. Inns were built to offer accommodations, and there is no doubt the proprietors felt that a good ghost story, especially a native romance, could help sell the location.

But people also seemed to sense some spirit in the ravine, something that existed long before storytellers tried to capture it. Many observers have noted that a mysterious force moves with the water as it emerges from its

Some have seen the spirits of both the mother and daughter in the falls, surrounded by a halo of butterflies. *Courtesy of Robert Oakes.*

source near the summit of Mount Washington and runs through the rugged, rocky gorge along the west side of the "Dome" mountain, plunging down the eighty-foot-tall falls and rolling into New York State, where it eventually empties into the Roeliff Jansen Kill and the Hudson River. Many journalists and local writers, like Joseph E.A. Smith and Willard Douglas Coxey, have tried to describe it. Painters like John Frederick Kensett of the Hudson River School sought to capture it in images. French tightrope walker Charles Blondin, who was famous for crossing Niagara Falls in 1859, felt drawn to perform a similar feat at Bash Bish, though it was reported he was more afraid of falling to his death there than he ever was at Niagara. In fact, many have been drawn there over the years, and some have indeed fallen to their death. This has led local authorities to institute strict rules against climbing and swimming.

What is it that has drawn so many to answer, as Smith wrote in 1879, "the hurrying summons…in the impatient roar of the cascade" to venture into what the *Hartford Courant*, in 1854, called an "exceedingly gloomy" and "dangerous" ravine? Apparently, this summoning force has been compelling enough to draw many thousands, despite the dangers and superstitions. "It is not so much the fall of water," wrote one *Pittsfield Sun* observer in 1844, "as the wild sublimity of the gorge that will strike you." And this "wild sublimity" just might inspire you to dream up stories of your own, like the tales of a ghostly face in a moonlit pool or of spirit voices in the rushing waters that call unwary travelers to the deep.

An Eerie Feeling in the Bones of Becket

According to a 2006 *Berkshire Eagle* article by Bernard A. Drew, a police diver once plunged into the pit at the heart of the former Chester-Hudson Quarry in Becket to explore it on behalf of the Becket Land Trust. He dove no deeper than twenty feet before he was scared off by what he found down there: a confused mass of twisted cables and broken gear left behind by the last quarrymen to walk off the site before it was abandoned and filled with water. Throughout the woods that surround the pit, those workers left hundreds of pieces of equipment scattered, including compressors, hauler trucks, winches, Sullivan drills, bull wheels, electrical generators and a massive fifty-five-foot-tall guy derrick that once hauled tons of heavy rock from the hole. They left, it is said, as if they were just breaking for lunch, but it was a break that has now lasted for more than fifty years. As the years have passed, the gear has rusted, and the forest has crept back in. Metal sheds and buildings have come down—vines and trees have grown up all around them—and huge heaps of blue-gray granite now await a transport train that will never come again.

Between its opening in the 1850s and its final days in the 1960s, the Chester-Hudson Quarry was the largest mining operation in the region and was a major contributor to the development of Becket and the surrounding towns. Much of the high-grade granite mined there was used to make monuments and tombstones that were shipped from nearby Chester and Hudson to locations throughout the country. The quarrymen used explosives, drills and derricks to extract the heavy stone. They hauled it out by horse and wagon until, in 1898, the Chester-Becket Branch Railroad was built for that purpose. When the railway closed in 1931, the quarrymen began using trucks like the ones that are now rusting among the other artifacts. Though business was booming, mismanagement reportedly forced the quarry's initial closure in 1946, after which it limped along until the 1960s, when it shut

As the years have passed, the gear has rusted, and the forest has crept back in. *Courtesy of Robert Oakes.*

down operations for good. Workmen simply walked off the grounds one day and never came back. Decades passed and nature reclaimed the quarry; it succumbed to slow, silent decay.

In 1999, a company called Labrie Stone Products sought to reopen the abandoned quarry, but a group of local citizens blocked the proposal, purchasing the three-hundred-acre property and donating it to the Becket Land Trust in order to preserve it for recreational use. Since that time, the Becket Land Trust Historic Quarry and Forest has offered hiking and cross-country skiing trails and a living museum dedicated to the region's industrial history. The quarry has also inspired more than a few reports of paranormal activity, earning it a place on numerous online lists of the most haunted hikes in New England. Some visitors have reported the eerie sounds of quarrymen still working the stone. They said they can hear distant voices and the noise of heavy machinery. Others have detected a strange, invisible presence and have felt the sensations of being watched and touched by something unseen. One hiker even reported being chased from the grounds by an angry spirit. A few claimed to have seen apparitions moving in a mist among the mounds of rock, and some others said they experienced electrical anomalies. Perhaps the strangest reports involve lights seen at night in the watery pit, "large-headed figures," a UFO and unexplained memory loss while at the site.

While walking among these rusted ruins and gnawed-out stones, it's easy to see how the quarry has inspired eerie feelings in the bones. For so long, men dug deep there, wrenching out the ancient rock from beneath the surface. Who knows what dark things may have been drawn out with it?

The Phantom Train of Pittsfield

There is something ghostlike about trains. They come to us from beyond—they pass us by and disappear again, into the unknown. That eerie, distant whistle, that ominous oncoming light and the sudden dark and silence that follow their passing—all of it seems otherworldly when seen from a certain point of view. Maybe this air of mystery explains why there have been so many stories about ghost trains over the years. The Berkshires has its own: the Phantom Train of Pittsfield.

The year was 1958, and the place was the Bridge Lunch Diner, which was formerly located at the intersection of North and Eagle Streets. In the tiny eighteen-seater, which was perched on the railway bridge at present-

From the overpass at present-day Sottile Park, many were startled to see a steam train barreling east down the track. *Courtesy of Robert Oakes.*

day Sottile Park, owner John Quirk and several lunchtime customers were startled by the sudden appearance of an old-fashioned steam train barreling east, toward Boston, down the seldom-used track. Witnesses reported seeing a baggage car, five or six coaches and a coal car so clearly that they could see the glowing embers. When reports of the incident started streaming in, railway officials insisted that no such train had run on the line that day. In fact, they said no steam engine had run through that region in years.

Nevertheless, one month later, witnesses again reported seeing a steam engine speed by the diner beneath the Bridge Street Overpass, and again, train officials dismissed the reports. But the story began to spread. Many said it was the ghost of a passenger train that collided with another in 1865, killing eleven. Others connected it to an 1893 incident in which a train bound for Boston was crushed by a collapsing bridge near Chester, resulting in the death of fourteen people. Wherever it may have come from, the spectral steam train did not reappear that year, and indeed, there have been no credible reports of sightings since 1958. But the story of the Phantom Train still echoes like a distant whistle through the Berkshire Hills.

THE SPIRIT SOLDIER OF FORT MASSACHUSETTS

On a small patch of grass in the parking lot of a now-empty Price Chopper Supermarket in North Adams, these words are written on a stone: "With gratitude to the defenders of the fort and to perpetuate the memory of the scene of their struggle in the wilderness." Long gone is the fort to which these words refer: the eighteenth-century English frontier garrison called Fort Massachusetts. The only indication that it ever stood there is a single stone chimney—the remains of a 1930s replica of the original structure.

Built in 1745, Fort Massachusetts was one of several English outposts constructed along the northern boundary of the colony to help protect frontier settlements against incursions by the French and their native allies and the Dutch settlers from New York. In 1746, during King George's War, French major Pierre de Rigaud de Vaudreuil and his force of nearly one thousand men captured and burned the meagerly manned fortress, and they marched their prisoners off to Canada. But in 1747, the fort was rebuilt. When, inevitably, the enemy returned, the better-defended second fort successfully repelled the attack.

The remains of the replica of Fort Massachusetts, near the now-empty Price Chopper Supermarket in North Adams. *Courtesy of Robert Oakes.*

There is reason to believe that the soldiers who struggled to defend the second Fort Massachusetts may have been helped by something other than sturdier walls and more reinforcements from nearby Fort Deerfield. According to a story told by Willard Douglas Coxey in his 1934 book, *Ghosts of Old Berkshire*, the second Fort Massachusetts was saved from capture and destruction by the spirit of Corporal Dimm, a soldier who had fallen during the attack on the first fort. As the enemy soldiers closed in on the outpost and capture again seemed imminent, the ghost of Corporal Dimm rose from his nearby grave and appeared on the ramparts, where bullets and arrows passed through his eerily illuminated body. "This was no ordinary sentinel," Coxey wrote. "He was too uncanny—too strangely transparent—to be of earth." The enemy was so horrified by the sight of this spirit soldier that they abandoned the attack and fled into the woods. Is there any historical truth behind this ghost story? While Coxey's account appears to be the only mention of a Corporal Dimm at Fort Massachusetts—either living or dead—who can say what spirit may have inspired those brave defenders to struggle against fear and overwhelming odds in the wilderness frontier of the early Berkshires?

THE GHOSTLY GUARDIANS OF GENERAL WASHINGTON

More terrifying than encountering a ghost alone on the road at night is encountering an entire regiment of ghosts—hundreds of them—marching in lockstep, silent as the grave. According to a story told by Willard Douglas Coxey in *Ghosts of Old Berkshire*, this is the very thing that happened one evening in April 1777 to a Berkshire farmer named Caleb Hudson. As Coxey tells it, Hudson "dashed into the taproom" of the South Lee Inn that night, "wild-eyed and nearly breathless, and staggered against the well-worn oaken bar…teeth chattering…eyes staring…[and] great beads of cold sweat on his face." As the landlord and other patrons listened in amazement, Hudson described his ordeal.

As he rode south from Lenox to Egremont, alongside the Housatonic River in South Lee, Hudson's horse stopped suddenly and sniffed the air, trembling and restless. On the road ahead, marching toward him from the direction of Stockbridge, Hudson saw what looked like a line of soldiers. As the Revolutionary War was underway at the time, Hudson thought it might be the British army on the move from New York or Connecticut, but

The Housatonic River in South Lee. Is this the place where Caleb Hudson saw the ghostly regiment cross? *Courtesy of Robert Oakes.*

as the men came closer, the frightened farmer could see by their uniforms that they were clearly Continentals. Then, Hudson was doubly afraid. Were those troops in the Berkshires that night to round up recruits for the Continental army? Hudson had no stomach for fighting, so he tried to hide as best he could as the ranks continued to advance toward him. Then, suddenly, just as they were about to overtake him, the soldiers turned off the road and, line-by-line, filed over the embankment and into the river ford, driven on by officers on horseback. It dawned on Hudson that this entire regiment of marching men, with hundreds and hundreds of booted feet, did not even make the slightest sound. None of the officers issued even a single command as the men, uncannily, turned in unison into the river. And when none of them appeared on the other side—when he was certain they had simply vanished in the night—Hudson knew he had encountered a regiment of ghosts. In a panic, his heart pounding, Hudson tried to turn his horse away, but the frightened creature bolted straight into the ford—right through the place where the ghosts had been and onward to the South Lee Inn.

Hudson chose not to tell his audience at the inn the true reason he had been out that night. He had been at a secret meeting of Tories, loyalists to the British Crown who opposed independence. They had gathered in the hills behind East Lee and hatched a plan to capture General George Washington, who was said to be at an encampment in Connecticut. Hudson never revealed his Tory affiliations to his fellow farmers, as doing so among so many Patriots would almost certainly have led to his arrest and, very possibly, his death. So, unknown to any but his fellow conspirators, Hudson was on his way that night to join up with a gang of Tories who were going to kidnap the general. Because of his encounter by the river ford, however, Hudson lost his nerve and gave up on the plot, which ultimately unraveled. Was it guilt that made Caleb Hudson imagine a regiment of ghostly troops that night, or were these truly phantom Continental soldiers who were so loyal to their general that they marched out of the underworld to stand between him and harm?

The Undead Hessian of Egremont

The story of the undead Hessian of Egremont may have been told since the late 1700s—the era in which it takes place—before Willard Douglas Coxey, in *Ghosts of Old Berkshire*, set it down as "The Ghost of Green River." According to the story, many residents of Egremont had claimed to see the spirit of a Hessian soldier named Franz Wagner, who had died while encamped outside the village. After burying his body in the town cemetery, his comrades continued their march toward Great Barrington. Not long after their departure, numerous villagers reported seeing an eerie apparition floating down the banks of the Green River, along the roads and among the tombstones in the riverside graveyard.

Determined to learn for themselves whether the Hessian's spirit did indeed walk among them, some men gathered together at the village store on a blustery night to warm themselves with a mug of hard cider before setting out to investigate. They were not gone long before they hurried back inside and sat down in stunned silence around the fire. Outside, the wind swept along the roads and through the trees, causing the walls of thin pine planks to creak and groan. A gust rose suddenly and pushed against the planks like an unseen shoulder pressing in, and all eyes looked nervously toward the windows and doors. When one of the men finally summoned up the courage to tell the storekeeper what he had seen in the cemetery that night, he described a figure dressed in a soldier's clothes, with long jackboots, a tall feathered hat and buttons shimmering in the moonlight. It rose up from one of the graves, spread its arms toward them and opened its mouth as if trying to speak. Then, it turned and floated slowly toward the river.

The men decided they would keep quiet about their experience that night. They knew it would only swell the panic many villagers already felt. At the time of the Revolutionary War, Egremont was a newly established town of farms and mills huddled close together on the banks of the Green River. The villagers would likely have felt anxious about the warring armies nearby—the Americans and the British, with their fearsome German auxiliaries, the Hessians. Throughout the revolution, King George III fortified his own ranks with these foreign fighters from Germany's Hesse-Cassel district, a region filled with tales of witches, goblins and fairies that later filled the pages of the Grimm Brothers' books. Many colonists thought these Hessians were cruel and merciless monsters, and they were all the more frightening because of the foreign language they spoke.

According to the story, Franz Wagner had been part of a regiment led by British general John Burgoyne who had lost a major battle just north of the Berkshires, near Saratoga. In 1777, Burgoyne had led his men south, from Canada into New York State, in an offensive designed to cut off all of New England from the southern colonies. But Burgoyne had underestimated the strength and size of the Continental army, which surrounded him and forced his surrender. While most of his troops were captured, some may have escaped, including, possibly, a small band of Hessians, who, according to the tale, set up camp beside Baldwin Hill, just outside the village. Their arrival would almost certainly have spread panic throughout the little farming community. It would have been enough to push the already-anxious villagers over the edge—enough to make a man afraid of his own shadow or to make him see ghosts.

In spite of the men's agreement to keep the sighting a secret, word spread quickly through the town, and with it came fear. Women and children stayed indoors after dark, and few men ventured out alone at night. The fear grew to a fever pitch as others began claiming sightings of their own. Many said they saw the ghost as they were crossing the river or passing the graveyard. One night, a young man named Cyrus Bright said that he and some friends, after waiting for hours in the graveyard, saw the hazy apparition rise from the grave and float away toward the river. They pursued the ghost along the water until it disappeared into the Devil's Den, a cave that was said to be used by thieves and fugitives.

Perhaps the most poignant account involved Widow Wister, a native of Germany who reported seeing the spirit outside her kitchen window and beside her bed. With sad eyes, it moved its lips as if to speak, but there was only silence. Was the Hessian homesick, drawn to Widow Wister because she spoke his native tongue? Was it looking for a friend among these foreign enemies? The local minister tried to soothe the restless spirit by placing flowers on its grave, but nothing could keep the Hessian's ghost from wandering.

At last, several of the villagers decided something needed to be done. No matter how unsavory the solution, they needed to restore the peace of

They saw the Hessian rushing toward them through the trees. *Courtesy of Katherine Oakes.*

Egremont. They decided that, if the Hessian was unhappy in their town, they would evict him. The plan was simple: gather in the graveyard, under the cover of night, dig up the body and carry it, by wagon, somewhere out of town. As the night deepened, the men traveled north on Van Deusenville Road with the rough wooden box that contained the Hessian's remains. Turning onto an old timber trail, they climbed Tom Ball Mountain just outside of West Stockbridge until the forest closed around them and they could go no further. Just then, a glint of pale light caught their eyes. There, on the coffin, sat the Hessian, dressed in faded regimentals, arms extended, mouth moving soundlessly. The men panicked, tripping over each other as they leapt to the ground. When they looked again, the ghost had gone, and so, hastily, they hauled the box into a hollow, dug a hole and lowered it down. As they tossed the last of the dirt onto the unmarked grave, they sighed, relieved to be rid of the Hessian at last—or so they thought.

As the men stumbled to the wagon, they looked back toward the lonely grave. And there, beneath the branches, in the dim light of the torch, they saw the undead Hessian rushing toward them through the trees. Terrified, they shrieked, leapt onto the wagon and whipped the horses. They raced back down the mountain and were home before first light. From that day on, the undead Hessian was never seen in Egremont again. But it was said that the residents of West Stockbridge became wary of the woods near Tom Ball Mountain.

2.
GHOSTS IN THE HOUSES

THE MOUNT

From the time she was a child, author Edith Wharton was troubled by ghosts—or at least by stories about ghosts. She read one such story while recovering from a near-fatal bout of typhoid fever, and it seemed to trigger a relapse that brought her back to the brink. She later recalled that reading this story plunged her into "a world haunted by formless fears," in which she felt there was a "dark, undefinable menace forever dogging [her] steps, lurking and threatening." And though Wharton was known, from her earliest days, as a great lover of books, she "could not sleep in the room with a book containing a ghost story," and she "frequently had to burn books of this kind, because it frightened [her] to know that they were downstairs in the library!" Did Wharton believe that these stories had the power to attract dark entities into her home? Was she anxious about the impression they may have made on her highly imaginative mind, with its "intense Celtic sense of the super-natural?" Given that Wharton felt such a fear of ghost stories, it is remarkable that she went on to write so many of her own. While she is best known for her society novels *The House of Mirth* and *The Age of Innocence* and her grim novella *Ethan Frome*, which is set in a fictionalized version of the Berkshires, Wharton also penned numerous supernatural tales during her career. Was she determined to face her fear of ghosts by writing about them?

The Mount beneath a dark and menacing sky. *Courtesy of Robert Oakes.*

It was not the first time that Wharton used her artistic gifts to free herself from unpleasant influences. While living in two different Victorian-style homes in Newport, Rhode Island, Wharton experienced symptoms of depression and anxiety. With their lack of symmetry and their dark, airless atmospheres, the houses themselves may have contributed to her poor mental health. So, in 1901, Wharton and her husband, Teddy, moved to Lenox, the "inland Newport," where many Gilded Age elites from New York and Boston were already building lavish summer cottages. There, Wharton drew on her knowledge of design and architecture to create a home that would be more soothing to her senses. Completed in 1902, the Mount was designed according to Wharton's aesthetic of balance, proportion and symmetry, which she called the "sanity of decoration." In this new atmosphere of light and airy spaces, there were very few places for shadows to linger, and Wharton's physical and mental health greatly improved. Her writing also flourished; she began her career in earnest during her decade at the Mount, and she produced several of her most highly regarded works there.

In spite of Wharton's efforts, it seemed a dark menace continued to dog her steps. During their time at the Mount, Teddy increasingly showed signs of mental distress. He often sank into moods of deep despair and flew into fits of agitation and anger. Although he had been known as an affable man who enjoyed the company of others, Teddy became more withdrawn as his behavior grew increasingly erratic. The marriage also suffered, as fights and infidelities led to a breakdown in trust and communication. So, in 1911, the Whartons decided to sell the Mount and part ways. Wharton moved to France, where she lived until her death in 1937, and Teddy remained in the town of Lenox, where he was laid to rest in the Church-on-the-Hill Cemetery in 1928.

Though she always remembered the Mount as her first true home, a work of art that she felt far surpassed *The House of Mirth*, Wharton moved on and created a new life for herself across the Atlantic. But in the woods of New England, her creation lived on and developed its own history, separate from that of its creator, witnessing many lives and at least one death within its walls. It served as a summer home for two private families until 1942, when it became part of the Foxhollow School for Girls until 1976. After several years of lying vacant, the Mount became the home of a theater group called Shakespeare & Company, which lived and performed there for two decades. In 1997, major restoration work began on the property, and shortly thereafter, the Mount officially opened its doors as a museum to celebrate the life and accomplishments of its famous creator. In recent years, the Mount has become a flourishing center of culture and community, enjoyed by many for its beauty.

But there is reason to wonder whether a dark menace remained at the Mount after the Whartons' departure, for as the years passed, the estate began to develop a reputation. People began to talk about its ghosts. Some of the earliest reports came from the students of Foxhollow School, who claimed to have conversations with the ghost of a woman in the cupola stairwell in the attic. According to the 1986 book *The Ghostly Register*, by Arthur Myers, another student said she witnessed an apparition in a white lace dress moving along the terrace and believed it to be the spirit of Wharton herself. In those years, she recalled, there were many rumors of the author's presence. Some claimed to hear her typing; others said every creak was Wharton walking the halls.

Years later, members of Shakespeare & Company reportedly witnessed some very dramatic sightings. According to the *Ghostly Register*, the company's founder, Tina Packer, described waking one stormy night to find the figure of a ponytailed man standing with his back to her in the center of the room. After calling out to him, she said, the figure turned and looked at her, and it was at that moment she knew it was a ghost. Frightened, she pulled the covers up over her head, and when she summoned the courage to look again, the figure was gone.

In the same book, another founding member of the company, Dennis Krausnick, reported a similar nighttime visitation; only his was more threatening. Krausnick said he woke to find a tall figure dressed in a hooded cloak standing next to his bed. He recalled being unable to see the figure's face, as the hood was drawn down over it. Though he tried to sit up, Krausnick said he was unable to move, as if something was holding him down on the bed. After some time, Krausnick said he was able to lift himself up, but by then, the vision had vanished.

Recently, Packer related another story involving Krausnick:

> *Dennis was the first person to stay overnight in the Mount. He was measuring rooms and wondering how many people we could house there. As he was working* [at dusk], *he heard footsteps on the top floor. He called up the stairs, but all was silent. He returned to his task, and again, he heard footsteps. This time, he went up to the top floor to look for whoever it was. But there was no one. Then, he started to get very scared. He slept that night in the car because he didn't want to be alone in the Mount.… On windy nights, it was often possible to hear the laughing of young girls coming from the tennis court on the other side of the square garden…and of course, the house itself was full of shadows.*

Since the days of Shakespeare & Company, there have been many reports of shadowy figures at the Mount. They have been seen in the main house, as well as in some of the outbuildings on the property. A number of years ago, a staff member discovered a workman sitting with his head in his hands beside the ticket booth. When asked what was wrong, the man said that, as he was working on the second floor of the stable, he saw the figure of a man crouching in the space just beneath the roof. The figure looked back at him with a piercing stare. The workman rubbed his eyes, hoping they were just playing tricks on him, but when he looked again, the thing was still there. According to the report, the workman was so upset by the encounter that he needed to take the rest of the day off.

One of the Mount's tour guides also needed some time to recover after reportedly witnessing a tall, slender, shadowy figure gliding toward her from the Henry James suite. And a cleaner who was working the graveyard shift once ran from the house, leaving the vacuum behind her on the stairs, after seeing an exceedingly tall form leaning out from one of the doors on the bedroom floor. The shadow of an unseen man was said to hover above a guide's shadow on the wall of Teddy Wharton's den. And another shadow figure, this one the silhouette of a woman, appeared in a photograph that was taken in the drawing room. One particularly striking feature of this apparition was that it seemed to have an unnaturally long neck and no lower body. Many photographs taken at the Mount have captured oddities, including orbs of light, shapes in mist clouds and more than a few faces in windows. Perhaps the most impressive of these photographs was taken by Shelly Negrotti in 2013. This haunting photo appears to show the strangely distorted face of a woman looking in through a window on the bedroom floor. Several other photos that were taken through this same window have also seemed to capture this phenomenon.

So many strange occurrences, including pats on the head, disembodied voices, sounds of footsteps and scents of cigar and pipe smoke, have been reported at the Mount over the years that it caught the attention of the Syfy Channel's *Ghost Hunters*. This team of paranormal investigators visited the

The pet cemetery on the grounds of the Mount, where the beloved Wharton dogs are buried. *Courtesy of Robert Oakes.*

estate twice, and each time, they found evidence that led them to conclude that there was, indeed, paranormal activity at the Mount. The sheer number of stories also moved the museum to begin offering its now-popular ghost tours, which have inspired many new tales of strange incidents that have been reported by the ghost seekers themselves.

It seems fitting that the home of a ghost story writer, who feared the genre and also seemed to relish it, should continue to inspire so many tales. If the "dark, undefinable menace" that haunted Wharton's imagination as a child did indeed follow her to the Mount, it has ultimately had a very positive effect. It has made storytellers out of the countless residents, employees and visitors who, like Wharton, have felt both frightened by and attracted to the disquieting delight of a good ghost story.

Ventfort Hall

One can imagine many reasons why ghosts might linger in a home. Maybe they do not know they are dead. Maybe unfinished business binds them to that location. Or maybe, while they were alive there, they experienced especially intense emotions that continue to resonate after their death. Maybe it's a powerful love or a heartbreaking loss that keeps them. Ventfort Hall in Lenox certainly witnessed its share of both.

One of the many "cottages" built during the Gilded Age, Ventfort Hall is an impressive twenty-eight-thousand-square-foot brick brownstone Jacobean Revival with twenty-eight rooms, seventeen fireplaces, a three-story wood-paneled great hall with grand staircase and its own bowling alley. Completed in 1893, the mansion was the summer home of George Morgan and his wife, Sarah, who was the sister of well-known financier J.P. Morgan. The Morgans had purchased the property in 1891 from sisters Annie Shaw and Clemence Haggerty. In 1853, their father, New York City businessman Ogden Haggerty, and his wife, Elizabeth, built a more modest Italianate villa there called Vent Fort, or "strong wind." It was so named because the absence of trees at the time made the grounds especially windswept. The Haggertys had enjoyed many tranquil summer days in their Berkshire home, but in 1863, that tranquility was shattered when the elation of young love was followed swiftly by the crushing blow of loss.

In May 1863, Annie married Colonel Robert Gould Shaw, the commander of the Fifty-Fourth Massachusetts regiment of African American soldiers.

Ventfort Hall has witnessed its share of love and loss. *Courtesy of Robert Oakes.*

The couple honeymooned briefly at Vent Fort before the young Union officer was called to South Carolina to lead his men into battle. Shaw left with fond memories of fleeting moments, hoping to return one day. As he wrote on June 1, 1863, while traveling south by steamship off the coast of Cape Hatteras, "I hope I shall never forget the happy days we have passed together, and that I shall always look back on them with the same pleasure as now. It may be a long time before we find ourselves driving about Berkshire together again, but I do hope that someday we can live over those days at Lenox once more." But that day never came. On July 18, 1863, as he led his men in a hopeless attack on Fort Wagner, Shaw was killed by Confederate gunfire. He was twenty-six years old.

A widow at age twenty-eight, Annie never remarried. When her father, Ogden, passed away in 1875, Annie, her mother and her married sister, Clemence Crafts, continued to spend summers at Vent Fort until they began renting the property to Flora and William Whitney, who later went on to build the Antlers on October Mountain. Elizabeth died in 1888, and Annie and Clemence passed in the early 1900s. Today, all of the Haggertys may be found buried beside one another in the Church-on-the-Hill Cemetery in Lenox.

After the Morgans purchased the property, they moved the original Vent Fort across the road, where it remained until it was lost to fire in 1965. When the new Ventfort Hall was completed, the Morgans celebrated with lavish housewarming parties. An article in the *New York Times*, published on September 17, 1893, mentioned that the Morgans "entertain considerably" and called Ventfort Hall "one of the finest Summer homes in the town." The Morgans must have been very proud of the estate. It was especially important to Sarah, whose home it truly was. "Sarah really loved the house," said Linda Rocke, the marketing director at Ventfort Hall Mansion and Gilded Age Museum. "It was her dream home."

Sadly, Sarah was only able to live her dream for a few short years. In 1896, her sudden death from a heart condition at age fifty-six shocked the Lenox community. She left the home to her children—Junius, George Jr. and Caroline—and she granted her husband the right to occupy the house for the remainder of his life. After mourning the loss of his beloved wife, George again sought love during his final years, marrying Sarah Learned Mifflin on Valentine's Day in 1899.

When their father died in 1911, the three Morgan children chose not to live at Ventfort and instead rented it to Margaret Vanderbilt, who suffered a tragic loss when her husband, Alfred, was killed in the sinking of the *Lusitania* in 1915. In 1918, Roscoe and Mary Bonsal took up residence in the home, renaming it Pembroke House, and they remained there until their deaths in 1933 and 1940, respectively. In the decades that followed, Ventfort Hall served as a dormitory for Tanglewood students, as a hotel called Festival House, as the Fokine Ballet Camp and as housing for a religious community called Bible Speaks.

The greatest threat to the survival of Ventfort Hall came in the 1980s, when a developer purchased the estate with plans to demolish it. Out of love for this historic property, the Ventfort Hall Association (VHA) formed in 1994 to raise the funds needed to save it. The VHA was indeed able to take ownership in 1997, but not before the estate suffered tremendous damage, including the loss of much of its original woodwork. There were also holes in the roof and floor, and an upper-level fireplace had fallen down into the basement. Undaunted, the VHA persevered and brought the beloved property back from the brink. By 2001, several of the rooms on the main floor had been restored, and the museum officially opened its doors to the public.

Reports of paranormal activity at Ventfort Hall began to emerge during the home's period of major restoration in the 1990s. According to Rocke, the spirits seemed to be more active during those years, likely stirred up by the construction work. Office manager Mark Monette said his first strange experience at Ventfort occurred in 2009. One night, at the end of his shift, after he had closed all the doors and switched off all the lights on the second floor, he returned to the main floor, where he heard the sound of booted footsteps coming from upstairs. He went up to investigate but found nothing. House manager Trevor Dean reported a similar experience. After shutting down the upstairs area, he said he also heard footsteps, as well as the sound of doors opening and closing on the second floor.

Other strange sounds reported in the house include dogs barking, whispers, screams and even a growl. Tour guide Nancy Whelan reported hearing soft voices on the main floor, as if two people were in conversation. And numerous paranormal investigators have captured what they believe to be the voices of entities that seem to be aware of their presence. Other peculiar phenomena have included messages transmitted by spirit boxes, which are devices that are said to allow ghosts to manipulate radio frequencies. During one investigation, it was reported that a spirit box was speaking the names of several of the people in the room and was inviting them to sit down at a table. While in Sarah's bedroom one night, investigators said they heard a voice in the spirit box command them to leave the room.

Strong smells have also been detected at the house. Common scents include flowers or perfume in Sarah's office and cigar smoke in the library and billiard room, places where George was often found. Women visiting the library have also reported the sensation of a hand brushing against them. Both men and women have said they felt a touch on the back or top of the head, and one staff member said he felt an affectionate touch on his back, as if the hand of a loved one gently stroked him. Numerous visitors have also reported cold spots in various places throughout the home.

Perhaps the most dramatic reports at Ventfort Hall are of the visual phenomena, including shadow figures, orbs, lights in the basement and actual apparitions. During the days of the ballet school, students said they often saw a woman dressed in the style of the 1920s following them up the stairs in the main hall, but when they turned around, she would disappear. Not long ago, a guest claimed to see a heavyset man wearing a tool belt standing at the top of the main stairs saying, "I'm too busy to talk." And recently, a spirit medium said she witnessed the figure of a woman following her through the halls, as well as the apparition of Mr. Morgan, who spoke to her, saying he would offer her a brandy if he only knew where it was. This medium, according to Rocke, believed that, though the spirits of both Sarah and George were present in the house, they could not find each other.

Could the spirits of Ventfort Hall be those of the Morgans reliving their Gilded Age glory days? Is it Robert Gould Shaw returning, at last, to relive those happy times with Annie? Or could it be Annie herself, or Margaret Vanderbilt, both bound to this place, where they suffered so much loss? Because so many people lived at Ventfort Hall throughout its history, it is difficult to say whose spirits may remain. And as the restoration work continues, it is anyone's guess as to how many more are yet to appear.

HOUGHTON MANSION

Gut-wrenching grief, guilt and the long-lingering shadow of tragedy have inspired many reports of unseen entities at the Houghton Mansion in North Adams. The mansion was once home to Albert Charles Houghton, the first mayor and leading citizen of this former mill town in northern Berkshire County. The son of a Vermont farmer, Houghton rose to prominence in the late 1800s as one of the most successful New England businessmen of his time; he was best known for running and revitalizing the Arnold Print Works, which was located at the current site of the Massachusetts Museum of Contemporary Art.

On nearby Church Street in 1897, Houghton built this seventeen-room neoclassical revival home, with mahogany-paneled walls and ceilings; Italian marble, onyx and rough stone fireplaces; white and gold-plated hardware; plate-glass windows; and a glass-enclosed sun porch looking out onto lawns and gardens. Intended to be a place where Houghton could enjoy happy times with his beloved family as he retired from public life, this majestic home came to bear witness to family catastrophe.

At 9:00 a.m., on August 1, 1914, Houghton, his youngest daughter, Mary, and family friend Sybil Hutton, along with her husband, Dr. Robert Hutton, set out from the mansion in Houghton's 1914 Pierce-Arrow touring car for a pleasure drive to Bennington, Vermont. At the wheel was John Widders, Houghton's chauffeur and coachman of forty-two years. Just outside the town of Pownal, Vermont, at about 10:45 a.m., the car climbed the steep and narrow Pownal Center Hill, which Houghton and his wife, Cordelia, had always dreaded, believing it to

A lingering shadow of tragedy haunts the Houghton Mansion. *Courtesy of Robert Oakes.*

be one of the most dangerous stretches of highway in the country. As they neared the brow of the hill, Widders swerved to avoid a team of workmen and inexplicably lost control of the vehicle. It plunged through a thin wire fence and down an embankment, overturning several times before landing in a nearby pasture.

Everyone, except Mary, was thrown from the car, which rolled directly over Sybil, crushing her head and killing her within minutes. Mary, with her face crushed and spine fractured, was brought to the North Adams Hospital, where she soon succumbed to multiple internal injuries. The men, though they sustained only minor bruises, cuts and broken bones, were deeply traumatized. After the loss of his beloved wife, Dr. Hutton was left speechless and shattered. Widders, who felt himself partly to blame, was absolutely inconsolable. He was reported to have uttered the words, "I wish it could have been me," all through the night following the accident. And though he was placed on suicide watch, it ultimately proved futile. At 4:00 a.m. on August 2, Widders entered the basement of the Houghton barn, put a revolver to his right temple and fired a single shot. His death, it was presumed, was instantaneous.

For Houghton, the shock of the ordeal, along with the death of his daughter and the suicide of his loyal employee, contributed to his swift decline and death ten days later in the master bedroom. The funerals for father and daughter were held at the Church Street home, and both, along with Widders, were laid to rest in the family plot at nearby Southview Cemetery. Sorrow and sympathy spread through the local community, as the entire city suffered this "appalling tragedy" along with its most prominent family. Businesses closed early, and black bunting was draped on the print works and the Main Street facades.

Mrs. Houghton lived out her remaining years on the same property where she had said goodbye to her husband and daughter and where the grief-stricken Widders had taken his life. When she died in 1918, Cordelia was buried beside her husband and daughter in Southview Cemetery. Several years later, the surviving Houghton children sold the mansion to an association of five Masonic orders, which built a huge two-story addition with lodge room and banquet hall, celebrating its completion in 1929 with a ritualistic dedication ceremony. For more than eighty years, the Masons continued to own and occupy the building until they sold it to a private investment group in 2017.

It was the Masons who first began to experience paranormal activity at the mansion "on a day-to-day basis," according to the Lafayette-Greylock Masonic Lodge Facebook page. The group experienced so many strange phenomena that, in 2004, it decided to start hosting investigations. Not long after, Mason Nick Mantello and his son Josh formed the Berkshire Paranormal Group (BPG) to run ghost hunts and other events at the house. In the time since the group's formation, the mansion's reputation as a haunted location has spread far and wide, attracting the attention of many ghost seekers, including the Travel Channel's *Ghost Adventures* and the Syfy Channel's *Ghost Hunters*. There have been numerous articles, books and websites dedicated to the ghostly history of the estate. Indeed, some consider it to be one of the most haunted houses in New England. It is important to mention, though, that the house is now under new ownership and is no longer open for paranormal events and investigations.

The reports of hauntings at the Houghton Mansion are many and varied. They include reports of cold spots and voices, shadow figures, footsteps and slamming doors experienced throughout the main house and temple addition. But the majority of reports seem to center on the basement and the third-floor servants' quarters. BPG members have seen shadow figures and strange light anomalies—which they call "sparklies"—in the basement, where they have also reported hearing laughter, which is believed to be that of a little girl who lived in the home that once stood in the same spot. Some have reported seeing this figure peeking out from behind a door, a phenomenon that appears to have been captured in an eerie video recently posted online by members of the Connecticut Paranormal Encounters and Research Group. Taps on the leg and tugs on hair have also been attributed to this entity, which some call a playful spirit, but others imagine something darker.

High above the basement, the third-floor servants' quarters also seem to be a hot spot of paranormal activity. There, BPG investigators reportedly witnessed a shadow figure appear in a doorway in the middle of the night and move across the room. Nearby neighbors have reported seeing lights on in this section of the house, though electricity no longer runs to these rooms. And a photograph taken by Josh Mantello seems to show the image of a figure peering out from one of the windows. Because John Widders once lived on that floor, many people believe it is his spirit that lingers there; some even claim to have seen him or to have heard his heavy footsteps on the back staircase that leads up to his room. Kindergarten teacher Lee Mullins, who ran an after-school program at the house, said she heard the footsteps one evening while waiting for a parent to pick up one of her students. When they heard the clear and distinct sound, Mullins and the child ran to the door, expecting to greet her mother. Yet, when they opened the door, no one was there. People have been known to feel intense sadness in Widders's chambers, and some have even been brought to tears. Another claimed to have recorded the voice of a man speaking about his heavy heart and felt sure it was Widders, who, because of the accident, had every reason to grieve.

In Mary's room, which is one floor down, visitors also describe feeling a deep sadness. Screams and sobs have been captured there, as well as voices speaking words like "get out." There have been footsteps detected and mist shapes and apparitions seen in that room, where a number of objects that once belonged to Mary were said to remain. When sitting in one particular chair, visitors often claimed to be touched by an unseen hand.

These and so many other strange occurrences at Houghton Mansion are attributed to the ghosts of A.C. Houghton, Mary and John, three victims of that harrowing accident so many years ago. Many believe the tragedy they suffered has left a lasting impression on the house, where Widders remains a prisoner of his everlasting guilt and shame and where Houghton and his beloved daughter Mary continue to mourn each other's loss and the loss of the happy life they once knew.

BUCKSTEEP MANOR

While hauntings are often attributed to tragedy or trauma, some seem to be echoes of pleasant times in peaceful places. This seems to be true of the ghosts that are said to haunt Bucksteep Manor in Washington.

Built in 1897 on land that had once belonged to Reverend William Gay Ballantine, Bucksteep Manor was the summer home of New York City attorney George F. Crane, who named the estate after an English castle that he and his wife often visited. In addition to the manor house and outbuildings, Crane also constructed an English-style walled garden and a Gothic Revival fieldstone chapel with a stained-glass window depicting St. Andrew, the chapel's namesake. There, on Washington Mountain, according to local historian Louise Elliot, Crane enjoyed the life of a gentleman farmer, with "a beautiful pair of matched bay Morgan mares whose dashes up and down the road were well remembered." The Cranes were also remembered fondly for their Christmas parties in the chapel and barn dances, which many local families were invited to. In 1927, Crane turned the house, along with 125 acres, over to the Episcopal Diocese of Western Massachusetts, which used it for many years as a recreational and conference center before selling the estate to Rudolph Sacco in 1971. For nearly forty-three years, the Sacco family operated a cross-country ski facility and family vacation center at Bucksteep. There, they hosted concerts, weddings and other events until they sold the estate in 2014 to a New York–based nonprofit.

Over the years, many strange occurrences were reported at Bucksteep Manor. Some said they heard creaking sounds and disembodied voices; others said they felt touched by an unseen presence. Still, others said they found objects that had moved, seemingly on their own. Such reports drew the attention of the Syfy Channel's *Ghost Hunters* in 2006. Though the investigation turned up little evidence, employees shared many personal experiences that left them feeling convinced of paranormal activity.

Heather Anello, whose mother started working at Bucksteep when she was very young, said she grew up hearing many stories about the place. Later, while operating a food service business there, she began having experiences of her own, which were mostly attributed to two spirits that she and other employees nicknamed "Seamus" and "Robert." Seamus, she said, was a short, plump figure dressed in robes or a hoodie that occupied the upstairs. Robert was the shadowy spirit of a tall, slender child that "lived" in a hole in a cellar wall. Anello said the spirit of Robert often twiddled her hair,

St. Andrews Chapel on the Bucksteep Manor grounds, where the ghost of a monk in robes has been reported. *Courtesy of Robert Oakes.*

something a psychic medium once told her the child often did with his own mother's hair when he was alive. Anello said she once discovered the figure of a man lying on a couch, though she knew that she was the only one in the building at the time. Another employee also reported seeing this same figure. Because the apparition in each instance seemed to be wearing a hoodie or robe, both women concluded that the spirit they had seen was Seamus, who was believed to have been a monk or priest in life.

Indeed, the most frequently reported ghost at Bucksteep Manor is that of a monk; it is said to walk the grounds and appear in doorways and windows. Anello said she once saw the monk peering through the kitchen door late one evening, but she could not make out a distinct face because the figure appeared to have something draped over it, like robes. Late one night, another employee said he was awakened by strange noises, so he walked downstairs, where he spotted the apparition of a man in a long brown robe pass through the door into Room 5. The daughter of a worker said she was terrified to see the figure of a man in brown robes standing outside the chapel as she and her mother passed by in their car. Who this monk might be is anyone's guess, but considering how long the property was used by the Episcopalians—and the fact that the manor was built on land that once belonged to Reverend Ballantine—it seems fitting that the most frequently seen ghost at Bucksteep is that of a holy man.

THE THADDEUS CLAPP HOUSE

During the height of the Industrial Revolution in the Berkshires, the Thaddeus Clapp House on Wendell Avenue was the heart of Pittsfield society. Built in 1871, this elegant ten-thousand-square-foot, three-story Colonial Revival, with twenty-five rooms and as many as twenty fireplaces was a warm and welcoming gathering place for the cultured and well-off, and it was presided over by businessman Thaddeus Clapp and his wife, Lucy. Though the home passed out of the Clapp family in 1906 and lived many other lives as a private residence, boardinghouse, apartment complex and bed-and-breakfast, many today believe that the house continues to be haunted by the illustrious Clapps and their ghostly guests.

In the waning years of the eighteenth century, the economy of the Berkshires was primarily agricultural, but the nineteenth century witnessed an explosive growth of industry and manufacturing in the county, with an influx of paper and textile mills, quarries, factories, iron foundries and glassworks, all coinciding with the introduction of the railroad. In Pittsfield alone, hundreds of mills employed thousands of residents and enriched several notable owners and operators, including Thaddeus Clapp, who was president of the Pontoosuc Woolen Mill on Keeler Street, near Pontoosuc Lake.

Clapp, whose father was one of the mill's founders, had decided to forgo college and, instead, immersed himself in the family business. As described in his obituary, which was published in the *Berkshire County Eagle* in 1890, "from his infancy, the sound of the waterfall and the clatter of woolen machinery had been familiar music to his ear, and…he found the attraction of the new Pontoosuc mill not to be overcome by those of the college twenty miles away." Yet, Clapp was also known as a man of letters who was "fond of amateur literary pursuits." In his youth, he had published his own homespun newspapers and campaign sheets, showing "that there was in him the making of a first-class editor by his writing." Clapp was also intensely interested in local history and was said to have the most extensive collection of "rare and curious old works regarding it than can be found in any other

Concealed behind walls and trees, Searles Castle is the perfect setting for tales of vengeful ghosts. *Courtesy of Robert Oakes.*

the 68,000-square-foot castle boasts seven towers, a two-story English oak-paneled great hall, a columned atrium and doors taken from Windsor Castle in England. Reports published not long after its construction called the castle "magnificent in its richness and its vastness," with elaborately decorated ceilings; silk, satin and tapestry-covered walls; delicately carved stonework above the entrance; imported marble and statues; and onyx wainscoting. Cutting-edge for its day, the estate featured a private electrical plant that powered lighting throughout the house and grounds. The centerpiece of the house was a massive floor-to-ceiling organ in the music room with controls that allowed musicians to adjust the lighting as they played in order to match the mood of the music.

Romance apparently blossomed between Edward and Mary as they worked together to design the home, and in 1887, they were married. But when Mary died only four years later, there were those who seemed unsatisfied by the official cause of death, which was reported in the *Chicago Tribune* on July 26, 1891, as "dropsy, which affected the heart…aggravated by an attack of the grip." Guards at the entrance of their residence and talk of a private midnight burial for Mary—along with rumors of Edward's growing eccentricity—led some to suspect foul play. Over time, a story grew of betrayal, murder and vengeful ghosts. As Mary became increasingly ill, it was said Edward began an affair with a household maid, whose quarters he would enter at night through a hidden staircase in the master bedroom. According to the tale, Edward and his lover lost their patience as they waited for Mary to die, so they killed her. Afterward, Edward and the maid continued their late-night trysts until, the story went, she tumbled to her death down the hidden staircase. He, meanwhile, was killed mysteriously by a falling chandelier.

The story persists to this day, appearing as recently as 2005 in *Weird New England*, by Joseph A. Citro, notwithstanding the fact that Edward Searles died in his hometown of Methuen, Massachusetts, in 1920. People also report seeing the ghosts of the unhappy threesome haunting the halls of the castle. And one *Berkshire Eagle* reporter, in 1962, wondered: "Do the file cabinets [of the firm that occupied the house at that time] get moved around in the night by the ghost of Edward F. Searles?" In addition to the specters of Edward, Mary and the maid, there are stories of a young boy who was killed when a tunnel beneath the property collapsed in the 1970s. People say his ghost now haunts the grounds and basement of the estate.

Concealed as it is behind walls and trees, "a castle snatched from fairyland," as it was once described, it's easy to understand why the Searles Estate has inspired such stories. With its towers and tunnels, secret doors and passages, it's hard to imagine a better setting for murder mysteries and ghostly visitations.

Ghost Houses

While several Berkshire houses may be haunted *by* ghosts, there are others that may be said to *be* ghosts. Where these houses once stood, only ruins or memories remain; yet, sites like Shadow Brook, the Antlers, the Mallery Homestead and Ashintully are still as much a part of the Berkshires as the Mount, Ventfort Hall and Naumkeag. Though they may be gone, their presence can still be felt.

Shadow Brook

Between the Civil War and World War I, many lavish summer homes appeared throughout the Berkshires, built by some of the most prominent and famously wealthy people in America. Each of these estates was a reach for the sky, but perhaps the most ambitious of all was Shadow Brook, an enormous one-hundred-room Tudor-style timber and stone mansion built in 1893 by New York City banker and businessman Anson Phelps Stokes. The home measured four hundred feet long and featured a circular tower, a red-tiled roof and several exterior porches. Regarded as one of the largest and finest private residences in the country, Shadow Brook was perched on a high hillside, looking out to Monument Mountain, Mount Everett and Mount Wilcox in the distance and down to the waters of the lake nearby.

Some said it was the home's nearness to this lake, known locally as the "Bowl," that led to the downfall of Shadow Brook. An article published in the *Wichita Daily Eagle* in 1903 refers to a popular superstition among local fishermen who spoke of "witchcraft that…bound the placid waters," causing the fish and other animals to behave strangely. The article goes on to blame all sorts of enchantments there on an "old Indian spell" cast by the last of the native people to be forced from their ancestral lands. There, beside the lake they called Mahkeenac, "they held wild and stormy pow-wows…[and] called down upon their evictors the curse that many believe is still working industriously against the paleface who invades the enchanted territory." The article suggests that this same curse inspired hauntings at the nearby Beckwith Estate, where the owner, Leonard Beckwith, later suffered a mental collapse.

The article also ties the curse to a series of mishaps at Shadow Brook, quoting Stokes: "My misfortunes…were many, and the chain of unusual circumstances which occurred there was strange, indeed." The most significant of these incidents was an 1899 riding accident that cost the avid sportsman one of his legs. No longer able to enjoy his rides and games of golf, Stokes chose not to return to the property. Instead, he rented it out for several years before selling it in 1906 to Spencer P. Shotter, who later lost his fortune in legal battles over alleged antitrust law violations. In 1917, Andrew Carnegie purchased the estate but was only able to enjoy it for a short time before he died in 1919. The mansion then housed a Jesuit novitiate until it was destroyed on March 10, 1956, by a massive fire in which three priests and a lay brother perished. With their home totally lost, the Jesuits chose to build a new novitiate not far from the vast, charred foundations. The Shadow Brook Novitiate remained

Shadow Brook burns. The massive estate was destroyed by fire on March 10, 1956. *Courtesy of the* Berkshire Eagle.

there until the 1970s. Today, that building is the home of the Kripalu Center for Yoga and Health, a place where many find spiritual solace and some even claim to feel the comforting presence of the priests who once lived there. In her 2008 book, *Berkshire Ghosts, Legends, and Lore*, E. Ashley Rooney refers to the spirit of a monk that is said to haunt the property.

It is remarkable that so many mishaps occurred in one location over such a short period of time. But if the stories are true, if they really were caused by a curse, it seems it may have lifted at last, as so many now find healing and comfort on the same grounds where Shadow Brook once burned.

The Antlers

Deep in the woods on October Mountain, there once stood a large, luxurious lodge known as the Antlers. It was the retreat of William C. Whitney, the secretary of the navy under President Grover Cleveland. Though Whitney already owned ten properties throughout the world, he had long dreamed of establishing his very own nature preserve where he could hunt wild game. So, in 1895, he began buying up thousands of acres of land in the so-called lone lands between Becket, Washington, Lee and Lenox. In all, Whitney acquired fourteen thousand acres in an area that measured roughly five by seven and a half miles square, making him the largest landowner in Massachusetts.

Many existing farmhouses—as well as a brickyard, sawmill and tavern—were abandoned, moved or razed in the land transfer, clearing the way for Whitney's hunting grounds and lodge. Whitney also built a stable, water and observation towers, camp houses and a lakeside boathouse and pavilion. In all, the estate was said to include twenty-four houses and thirty barns, along with miles of roads and paths. But the true marvel of the estate was a one-thousand-acre enclosure where Whitney kept wild buffalo, elk, antelope, rare black-tailed deer and a pair of Canadian moose. He also stocked the ponds with fish; bred pheasants, partridge and quail; and kept angora goats, sheep and Belgian hares.

Whitney had realized his dream, but he was not able to live it for long. He enjoyed only a few two-week stints at the property over a handful of years before he died in 1904 at the age of sixty-two. Whitney's children had no desire to maintain the property, so the buildings deteriorated. The animals were either sold to zoos and other preserves or escaped to fend for themselves. One escapee, "Old Bill" the moose, became quite famous, as reports of sightings of him grew throughout the region. Some even said they spotted the legendary beast walking down the Main Streets of Lee and Lenox.

In the 1920s, the Antlers was lost to fire, and the property ultimately became the October Mountain State Forest. Today, hikers, hunters and nature lovers all enjoy this lush wilderness, though many believe it is a hot spot of paranormal activity. Strange stories date back to the years just after Whitney's death. One article published in the *Boston Globe* on December 27, 1908, describes a hunter's harrowing encounter with enormous bats, which he called "the vampires of Berkshire." The hunter, Peter J. Tyer of Lenoxdale, said that he had been fishing on Finnarty Pond when a sudden and terrific thunderstorm swept in. The sky turned inky black as rain came down in buckets and lightning lit up the lake. Tyer made it back to camp, where he found his horse neighing wildly, eyes bulging and feet stamping; he was "crouching low and trembling like a leaf." Later, as Tyer blew out his lantern and lay down to sleep, the horse began to lurch and whinny. He reached out to stroke the animal's neck, only to find it covered with bloody gashes, several near the throat, "as though stabbed with a sharp knife."

Then, Tyer saw "birds as large as crows sweeping backward and forward, but strange to say, although [he] could feel the wind from their wings…as they swept down near [him] and [his] horse, there was not a sound to be heard." As daylight broke, Tyer said he could see clearly that these were no birds, rather they were "monster bats, or vampires, measuring at least 14 inches or more across the wings."

Vampire bats are not the only strange creatures said to inhabit October Mountain. Stories persist of "horned devils" seen near Felton Lake, as well as a huge "humanlike" creature with glowing eyes reportedly seen in 1983 and again in 1989. Some say these are only the descendants of Whitney's big game escapees still roaming his former nature preserve. But others believe they are something supernatural. They also say that Whitney himself haunts his old estate. They say that, with a lantern in his hand and a dog by his side, his spirit moves from tree to tree, apparently on the eternal hunt for infernal big game.

The Mallery Homestead

If you drive along Mallery Road in New Ashford, you will find the bones of the town's first home at the edge of a private residence. In the center of a cellar hole surrounded by a carefully manicured lawn stands a substantial stone chimney—the only remains of the Mallery Homestead, which was built in 1794 by town father Uriah Mallery. The wooden structure that was once supported by those stones succumbed to a fire on December 16, 1930, but it was an event that occurred there seventy years prior that laid it low in the eyes of locals and made many afraid to go near it at night.

On the evening of July 29, 1861, two blood-soaked bodies were found lying on the floor of the upstairs bedroom, both with gashes across their throats. The woman, Eunice Vanderwarker Pratt, who was seventeen, was dead; her husband, Henry, who was twenty-one, lay gasping and gurgling. They had only been married for three weeks; they had run away from their home in Osceola, New York, to try to start a new life together in the Berkshires. But when Eunice's father, Mr. Vanderwarker, came after her and found the young lovers living on the Mallery Estate—then owned by Uriah's grandson, Van Ness—he confronted the couple. He tried to convince young Eunice to come back home with him, but she refused, saying Henry—who was, in fact, her uncle—was kind to her. According to an article in the December 28, 1930 edition of the *Springfield Sunday Union*, Pratt and Vanderwarker exchanged

Some have claimed to hear howling voices in the Mallery House chimney, pictured here in 1955. *Courtesy of Warren Fowler,* Berkshire Eagle.

angry words, and the young man shook his fist in the air. Eunice was heard saying that she would rather die than return home. Then, Pratt put his arm around his bride and whispered in her ear, and the two ascended to the second floor. Minutes later, Vanderwarker, Mrs. Mallery and others made the gruesome discovery: a murder-suicide attempt that succeeded in killing only Eunice. Pratt survived to face trial, and though he was condemned to die by hanging, his sentence was commuted to life in prison. When asked why he did it, Pratt replied, "She wished us to die together."

In the years that followed, the Mallery House developed an eerie reputation. Subsequent occupants claimed to see lights, ghosts and skeletons inside, and indelible bloodstains were said to appear on the second floor. Phoebe Jordan, who lived on a neighboring farm, was quoted in the *Union* article as saying that she remembered seeing blood in the home "which never could be washed off." Others claimed to see faces peering out of the upstairs windows, and they heard the sound of howling voices, believed to be those of Eunice and Henry, emanating from the chimney. Local children kept their distance, especially at night, as they were afraid to encounter the phantoms in the fireplace.

Today, the stones are quiet, and the site is peaceful and picturesque. Perhaps the fire of 1930 purged the place of its mournful ghosts and the bloodstains of the desperate lovers that could never again come clean.

Ashintully

Of all the ghost houses in the Berkshires, Ashintully may be the most mysterious. This huge thirty-five-room Palladian mansion—known as the Marble Palace—was built in 1912 by politician and Egyptologist Robb de Peyster Tytus and his wife, Grace. Against the green brow of Round Mountain, at the foot of Tyringham Valley, Ashintully's marble, stucco and white sand walls were said to sparkle in both sunlight and moonlight. Locals and tourists alike often passed by just to goggle at it. But visitors today see no grand palace with high vaulted halls or two-story library with twelve thousand volumes; instead, they find four cracked Doric columns standing on the charred and weedy stone foundation—all that remains after a fire took the rest on April 22, 1952.

Tytus built the home as a wedding gift to his wife on the more than one thousand acres of farmland they had purchased in 1903. It was to be a place where the couple could entertain guests and experience the joys of luxurious country living. Ashintully also came to house the ancient artifacts that Tytus had brought back from Egypt's Valley of the Kings, including a wall frieze from the palace of Amenhotep III, the grandfather of King Tutankhamen, and even a three-thousand-year-old mummy. Though Tytus was famous for his Egyptian excavations, local residents seemed surprised to learn he had been bringing his acquisitions back to Tyringham. Newspapers in 1911

Four cracked columns on a weedy stone foundation are all that remains of Tyringham's Marble Palace. *Courtesy of Robert Oakes.*

reported the shock of workmen who made the discovery of a body in a barn on the property. The men alerted the sheriff, who summoned a local doctor, who determined that the man in question had been dead for more than three thousand years. Apparently, Tytus had stored a mummy in the barn, intending to move it to the main house once it was completed.

Other relics Tytus brought to Ashintully from the palace of Amenhotep III included a necklace of semiprecious stones and a cosmetics container made from some of the oldest glass in existence. Tytus also kept other rare and valuable objects, such as a cup used by Bonnie Prince Charlie, parchment books and paintings from the 1500s, eighteenth-century Irish amethyst glass and some of the earliest Waterford crystal ever made. Perhaps the Marble Palace in the Tyringham Valley was Tytus's attempt to emulate the palaces in the Valley of the Kings, going as far as to furnish it with objects that once belonged to those ancient sovereigns.

But sadly, Tytus was not able to enjoy his majestic estate for long. Months after Ashintully's completion, at the age of thirty-eight, the famed Egyptologist died of tuberculosis. Tytus's death was the first in a series of misfortunes that led some at the time to believe that the family was cursed by the ancient Egyptian pharaohs. In 1928, Grace died suddenly of a pulmonary embolism at age fifty-three, and five years later, their daughter, Mildred, was killed in an automobile accident while driving home from the estate; she was twenty-eight. An article written by John B. Knox in 1951 alluded to the persistent rumors among the superstitious that "the family had incurred the displeasure of Egypt's dead kings by disturbing their sleep." When the estate burned to the ground less than one year later, it must have seemed to them like a confirmation of this rumor.

One other strange incident that is said to have occurred at Ashintully was mentioned in an article in the *New York Times*. According to that report, author Henry Adams, the great-grandson of President John Adams, said he was awakened one night by a voice speaking his name. Then, a portrait that hung on the wall at the foot of his bed started to glow and "for a few minutes conversed with him" until he drifted off to sleep. Mildred Tytus, who related the tale, said she believed the painting, unbeknownst to her father, had been stolen from a Roman palace and smuggled in among other objects he had purchased. Although Tytus had tried to return the painting to its owner, it was never claimed. Adams said he heard the voice often during his time at Ashintully, but no one else was ever known to experience the strange phenomenon.

3.

GHOSTS AT THE INNS

THE GHOSTLY GUEST IN 301: THE RED LION INN

With its grand porch and cozy parlors, leafy courtyard and lively downstairs den, the Red Lion Inn is one of the most iconic Berkshire landmarks, a venerable establishment on the corner of Main and South Streets in Stockbridge, where an inn has stood since before the American Revolution.

In 1773, when Main Street was little more than a dusty coach road, Silas Pepoon established a small tavern on this spot; it served travelers and, sometimes, early revolutionaries who gathered there to voice their anger over British injustices. In 1873, Mr. and Mrs. Charles H. Plumb took up ownership and filled its rooms with much of the antique furniture and china that is still found there today. In the waning years of the nineteenth century, the Stockbridge House, as it came to be known, flourished until tragedy struck on August 31, 1896, when a devastating fire destroyed the entire building. Incredibly, the inn was rebuilt, and its doors were reopened less than one year later. In the years since its miraculous rebirth, the Red Lion Inn has remained one of the most popular and recognizable Berkshire guesthouses, hosting five U.S. presidents and many other notable guests, like Nathaniel Hawthorne, William Cullen Bryant, Henry Wadsworth Longfellow, Thornton Wilder, John Wayne, Carol Burnett, Paul Newman, Steven Spielberg, Leonard Bernstein and Bob Dylan.

The Red Lion Inn's most notorious guest is the ghost that is said to haunt Room 301. *Courtesy of Robert Oakes.*

But perhaps the inn's most notorious guest is the ghost said to haunt Room 301, a cheerful little room at the end of the third-floor hallway. It is this ghostly resident, along with other reported apparitions and occurrences, that make the Red Lion Inn a favorite haunt of paranormal investigators and psychic mediums. A glance at an online travel site reveals a number of eerie accounts that are said to have occurred in Room 301, including reports of sheets and toes tugged, gentle touches of the head and face, scratches on the hand and even an unseen entity entering the room and climbing into bed. More than one reviewer also mentioned seeing an apparition of a man in a top hat.

Over the years, a number of paranormal investigators have sought to verify these claims. Berkshire folklorist Joe Durwin, who writes about local mysteries on his blog *These Mysterious Hills*, once checked himself in to the infamous Room 301 to conduct his own investigation. During the night, he claimed he experienced "certain electrical fluctuations" while using an EMF detector, which revealed "high spikes" between the bed and armoire. Another pair of ghost investigators, Joseph Flammer and Diane Hill, who are also called the Paranormal Adventurers, also reported odd anomalies and unexplained phenomena while staying in Room 301. They claimed that a video camera that was left running through the night recorded eighteen distinct knocks, mostly emanating from the armoire. They claimed that a camera also captured a hazy figure that moved past the mirror at 2:00 a.m. and that "something" else crossed the room and struck the camera's tripod. The dowsing rods they were using at one point crossed above a cold spot, and a question they posed to the darkness—"Is there a spirit here in the room with us?"—seemed to be answered by knocks from inside the armoire. At one point, they said, its doors actually began to creak open on their own.

While Room 301 does appear to be an especially active room, reports of strangeness at the Red Lion Inn are not confined to that location. In Room 424, for example, one guest reported feeling that something was standing over her bed. Another guest asked to be moved to a different room because of the many disturbances he experienced during the night. Others have claimed to see the apparition of a girl with flowers in her hand. Another visitor said she felt an unseen hand brush against her while walking down the stairs into the first-floor parlor. And according to a former housekeeper, much of the cleaning staff believes the entire fourth floor of the inn is haunted.

So, how does the management of the Red Lion Inn feel about all of these reports? They seem to enjoy the mystery of it all. In response to the question of whether the inn is haunted, they wrote on their website, "After 235 years… that's a lot of guests…and old buildings do make strange noises…so there are a lot of rumors and stories. Are they true? Why not decide for yourself. And let us know if you see anything."

THE KNOX TRAIL INN

Long before the first town was established in the Berkshires, there was a road; it spanned the inhospitable woodlands between Albany and Westfield and traveled onward toward Boston. Native Americans and European fur traders walked it, so did the first hearty settlers, who were seeking a means of access to the rugged, rocky wilderness. Soldiers who had fought in King Philip's War, the French and Indian War and the Revolutionary War also marched this main route through the southern Berkshires. Throughout its long history, this road has been known by many names: the Great Road, the New England Fur Trail, the Post Road and the Greenwoods Road, among

Do the ghosts of Knox's men haunt the land beside the Knox Trail Inn? *Courtesy of Robert Oakes.*

others. But today, it is called the Knox Trail in honor of General Henry Knox, who led an arduous wilderness trek along this road during the winter of 1776 to transport artillery to Boston from the fallen Fort Ticonderoga, resulting in a decisive American victory over the British.

Along the way, Knox and his men would have passed through the small farming settlement of Louden, which is known today as Otis, though not past the Knox Trail Inn, which was not built until 1820. Nonetheless, since at least 1935—when Clifford and Jennie Clark bought the property and changed its name from the East Otis Hotel to the Knox Trail Inn—the owners of the establishment have proudly celebrated its proximity to this significant historical landmark.

Owners and patrons alike have also reported strange experiences at the inn that have led many to believe the building is haunted. Much of the local lore focuses on the spirit of a soldier known as Jake. Some say he fought in the Revolutionary War, while others associate him with the Civil War; still, others say he served during World War I. One patron claimed they saw this apparition standing near the fireplace in the Pine Room and described it as a man in a Revolutionary War–era uniform with his head and neck covered by bloodied rags. But Beverly Murphy, whose family owned and lived at the inn from 1977 until 1986, recalled a more contemporary figure.

Waking one night in her room on the second floor, Beverly said she saw the spirit of a blond-haired, slender young man in a green World War I–era military jacket appear at the window near her bed, turn and walk toward her and then vanish. Beverly's brother Tim said he once caught a glimpse of a ghostly arm reaching out from the service window in one of the barrooms; it, too, appeared to be wearing a green World War I military jacket. The Murphy matriarch, Karen, said she once saw this same figure in the Pine Room. After hearing a noise in there one night, Karen said she burst in, expecting to find local kids trying to steal booze from behind the bar. What she found instead was "a blond kid with an army jacket looking into the fireplace at the white stone that's there, just looking at it." She continued, "I said, 'I gotcha now,' but then, he moved toward the door and disappeared." Karen said she once noticed a similar-looking young man in a photograph that was taken around the time the inn was built, leading her to wonder whether this might have been the same man. "I think it was him," she said, "but it was hard to tell. Everything happened so fast."

"Weird stuff always happened," said Beverly. "Every night, at 4:00 a.m., we heard pacing and creaking in the attic. It woke everyone up." Beverly said they could always feel when the spirit was in the room because there would be cold spots. However, she said nothing about the experience was disturbing. "It always felt comfortable. You knew you were never alone. He was always there. He didn't want attention. He just wanted to be part of everything." In fact, the spirit became so much a part of the Murphy family that Karen began to treat it as one of her kids; she once even scolded it for bad behavior. "One night, my husband was late coming home," she said. "There was a storm outside, so I closed up and went up to bed. I came down later and all the candles were lit in the front barroom. I blew them out and then went back up to bed. When I came back down a little later, they were all lit again. I said, 'Stop it! You're gonna burn the place down!'" And it stopped.

But in recent years, it seems that Jake has become more mischievous and less obedient. There have been reports of electrical anomalies, cold spots, disembodied voices and shadow figures on the property. According to one report, a jukebox once turned on and began playing a song that it did not even contain. One patron claimed to see plates tossed by an unseen hand and toilet paper unrolling on its own. Another said he awoke in the night to discover a face hovering over him. A paranormal investigator claimed to have his shirt tugged and lifted while exploring the attic. According to general manager Bethany Perry, the spirit likes to play pranks. These pranks include pulling aprons and tugging on hair, and once, she said, as she tried to convince a skeptical friend that the place was haunted, the ghost threw a water glass down on the floor between them. "Yeah, he likes to torture Bethany," joked Beverly.

Given that the Knox Trail Inn did not exist during the Revolutionary War, it seems unlikely that these hauntings have anything to do with Knox and the famous trail that bears his name. Still, how do we explain the reported sightings of a Revolutionary War soldier, as well as the sound of spirit soldiers dragging something heavy past the inn, which others have reported? While the Knox Trail Inn may not have housed those hearty Patriots more than two hundred years ago, could a memory of their procession remain in the land on which the current structure stands?

THE NEW BOSTON INN

The New Boston Inn is old; it's likely the oldest inn in Berkshire County. Perched on a rise beside the Farmington River, where Routes 8 and 57 intersect, this quaint country hotel has welcomed weary travelers for more than two hundred years. While the main portion of the building was erected circa 1800, the tavern in the west-side ell dates to the 1750s, when New Boston Village in present-day Sandisfield was set to become a bustling stagecoach stop along the way from Hartford to Albany. Over the years, it has witnessed a rise and fall in fortunes and has changed hands many times. It has been altered, enlarged and restored repeatedly, but it has always been an inn.

Many famous guests have stayed here through the years, including Anne Lindbergh, Liz Taylor, Richard Burton, Bing Crosby, James Thurber, Pearl S. Buck and Agatha Christie. But the inn's most famous guest is said to be a ghost named Harriet, the supposed cause of the many strange sights and sounds reported here for years. According to local lore, Harriet was the daughter of a well-off family from New York City who summered at the inn during the early years of the nineteenth century. One summer, she fell in love with a local farm boy who wanted to marry her but was spurned by her parents, as they knew this poor farmer would never provide the kind of

A bride killed by her jilted lover may haunt the New Boston Inn. *Courtesy of Robert Oakes.*

high-society life their daughter was accustomed to. They dragged Harriet, broken-hearted, back to the city and arranged for her to marry a man of means, while the spurned suitor enlisted in the army and left the farm to fight in a war.

The following summer, Harriet returned to the inn with her family and new fiancé. Cruelly, she was to marry the man she felt nothing for in the same place she and the farmer had found true love. But that love turned to jealous rage when the farmer-turned-soldier learned of the plan. He ran to the inn, burst into the second-floor ballroom and, before all the gathered guests, demanded the wedding to stop. When Harriet told him that the ceremony had already taken place, that she was already married, the farm boy drew a revolver, shouting, "If I can't have you, no one can!" And he shot his dearest love in the stomach. Bleeding, Harriet stumbled across the ballroom floor, out to the hallway and into one of the bedrooms, where she fell down dead. The next day, her killer was hanged from a tree near the inn. For years afterward, no one could scrub Harriet's blood from the upstairs ballroom floor.

Very little historical evidence exists to support this account. There appears to be no mention of it in the newspapers or burial records from the time; yet, the story persists. Indeed, many people, including guests, innkeepers and staff, have claimed to encounter Harriet's ghost at the inn. They have sensed her presence in the sound of footsteps or in a disembodied voice that always sings the same tune, identified by one investigator as a popular wedding song from the early 1800s. Objects have been seen moving around on their own, doors have opened and closed, door handles and locks have been seen turning and water faucets have started running. According to one report, all of the fire alarms in the building were inexplicably triggered once during a wedding and would not stop even after the system was disconnected from its power source. There have been reports of objects, like garments and jewelry, mysteriously going missing, only to reappear later in plain sight. A phantom face was once seen looking through a bedroom window on the second floor. Guests have complained about the sound of music and dancing emanating from the ballroom, and comments in the guest book have mentioned strange noises in the empty bedrooms at night.

The current owner, Barbara Colorio, has reported feeling comforted by the spirit of Harriet, which she has said she experiences as loving and even whimsical. The report of Colorio's entire collection of music boxes all starting to play at once one night certainly suggests a playful presence. But one account involving a former innkeeper hints at a less gentle entity. A column by Robert Rushmore in the August 17, 1976 issue of the *Berkshire Eagle* describes former owner Virginia Strong as "looking pale and shattered and marked by a classic black eye. She had fallen, it seemed, down the long flight of stairs from the ballroom." When pressed by Rushmore about whether or not she would go through with the sale of the inn, as she had been considering, Strong said, "Certainly the ghost doesn't want me to sell. That's who pushed me down the stairs, you know."

Former employee Francis Deming, in the October 2011 issue of the *Sandisfield Times*, described a very eerie incident involving young children who apparently saw something no adult could see. While babysitting guests' children on two different occasions, Deming wrote that she heard them talking to someone unseen in the sitting room. When asked who they were talking to, the children replied, "The blue lady with no feet." Deming also wrote about experiencing the wispy figure of a young girl in white in the front hall, a rocking chair in the ballroom rocking on its own and coming to a sudden stop, a dog suddenly lifting its head to watch something unseen move through a room and unexplained clattering and creaking floorboards when no one else was in the building.

A number of paranormal investigators, including those from the Syfy Channel's *Ghost Hunters*, have explored the inn in recent years. While *Ghost Hunters* was unable to capture compelling evidence—with the possible exception of a pen that seemed to write and move on its own—other groups have captured images of what they claim to be apparitions and a recording of what they believe is a female voice calling faintly through static, "I'm here."

It is not surprising that a place as old as the New Boston Inn should inspire more than a few accounts of ghost sightings. And because so many people have slept and dined and danced under its roof, it really is anybody's guess whose spirits these may be. But the story of a jilted lover and the young woman he killed in a fit of jealous rage continues to capture the imagination of many local residents and visitors.

WHISTLER'S INN

Can a house cry? Maybe if it's haunted by heartbroken ghosts. Some say that three such spirits haunt Whistler's Inn in Lenox, where two sisters and the man they both loved once lived together, entangled in a net of betrayal and forbidden desire. In the years since their deaths, some have blamed flooded floors and burst pipes on these weeping, lovesick spirits.

Built in 1870, across from the Church-on-the-Hill Cemetery, this Tudor Revival house was originally known as Hillside and was the summer residence of Mrs. Hartman (Grace) Kuhn. After Mrs. Kuhn died in the house in 1908, industrialist Ross Whistler, the nephew of renowned painter James Abbott McNeill Whistler, and his wife, Theo, purchased the property, renaming it the Hidden House. After Ross's death in 1927, Theo hired Swedish beauty queen Nancy Hedwall to serve as her live-in maid and household companion. Nancy soon asked Theo to allow her sister Helma and Helma's husband, Paul Anthony, to join them in the sprawling fourteen-bedroom mansion, claiming to need help with its upkeep. But as the story goes, Nancy had a hidden motive, as she was in love with Paul Anthony. Soon after Paul and Helma moved in, Paul began meeting with Nancy behind his wife's back, often in the carriage house or upstairs in the attic. This continued until Paul died suddenly, in spite of his youth and good health; this led some to suspect

Does a threesome of lovesick ghosts still linger at Whistler's Inn? *Courtesy of Robert Oakes.*

murder, while others said he was simply worn out. The sisters continued living at the Hidden House in the service of Mrs. Whistler, and when they died, they were buried beside Paul Anthony across the street.

As reported in the *Berkshire Eagle*, Richard Mears, whose family has owned and operated Whistler's Inn for more than fifty years, first began noticing the mysterious appearance of water in the building as far back as 1974. After the death of his uncle Elton, who had previously owned the inn, Mears came to stay for several days that winter to do some maintenance on the property. At the time, the water and heat were shut off, and the house was so cold that icicles hung from the ceiling. Mears reported that, while passing through a hallway to one of the upstairs bedrooms, he discovered that the hallway, which had been dry moments before, was covered by an inch of water. Given that the house was frozen and the water was turned off and given that there was neither rain nor any open windows, Mears could not explain the water's appearance. This sudden flood was just the first of many strange events involving water at the inn. Pipes have burst, puddles have appeared and liquid has been seen cascading down a wall, into the kitchen sink, then down into the basement directly to the sump pump, resulting in surprisingly little damage. Interestingly, these events often occurred just as Richard was about to leave the house for an extended period of time. According to an article by Jack Dew in the May 18, 2003 issue of the *Berkshire Eagle*, Richard's wife, Joan, said she believed the water was the tears of a spirit that was so in love with him it wept to see him go.

These water-related events are not the only odd phenomena that are said to occur at Whistler's Inn. Exploding windows, electrical surges, cold and warm spots, disembodied voices and flickering lights have all been reported there. Innkeepers and guests alike have seen female apparitions, which are believed to be either Nancy or Helma. One guest reported seeing the ghost of a woman standing over her and staring down at her as she lay on her bed. Others have reported a male presence that they believed to be either Ross Whistler or Paul Anthony.

Several of the bedrooms in the house are said to be haunted, in particular, Rooms 1, 5, 7 and especially 12 (the attic). There, guests have reported waking in the middle of the night to find a tall, shadowy figure standing over them. Some have said they felt as though there was something up in that room that did not want them around. Joan reported hearing the voice of a woman in the attic whisper, "Go away. We want to be alone." This led her to wonder whether the spirits of Nancy and Paul continue to sneak up there for secret trysts in the afterlife.

4.

GHOSTS IN THE GRAVEYARDS

In the Berkshires, the dead are everywhere. Drive through any of the thirty-two towns in the county, and it won't be long before you come upon a graveyard. Some are next to the road, but others are hidden away, beneath trees or on a hilltop. Some are modern; others, with their eerie winged skulls and grim, faded inscriptions, date back to the earliest settlements. Still, others are invisible; the markers are now long gone—if there ever were any there. And yet, the dead remain.

If you pull over for a moment and take a walk among the tombstones, a peculiar feeling may come over you, a powerful pull toward the past or a palpable connection to lives once lived. You might feel it as a presence, something unseen behind a stone, beneath a tree or in the glass of a mausoleum door. You might even think you see something there, especially in the twilight when you are alone. While there haven't been many reports of actual apparitions in Berkshire graveyards, there have been a few worth noting. And in several cases, these unusual cemeteries and their notable residents are stories themselves.

NATIVE AMERICAN BURIAL GROUNDS

One cannot talk about the graves of Berkshire County without mentioning the burial grounds of the Mohican people, whose home this once was. Long before the first European settlers moved into the region, indigenous people

The stone monument at the site of a Mohican burial ground at the west end of Main Street, Stockbridge. *Courtesy of Robert Oakes.*

lived and died here, burying their dead on sacred land, much of which has since been disturbed by development. In his 1882 book, *History of Great Barrington*, Charles J. Taylor refers to the natives' "many places of interment" throughout the region, describing one such place "in the extreme north part of Sheffield" and another "in Great Barrington, on the east side of the highway and just north of the Agricultural Ground," where a large number of bodies were exhumed during the excavation of a sand bluff. Taylor went on to say that one man, while "digging a cellar, came upon two Indian skeletons…[and] a mile south of the village, the remains of six bodies were disinterred" by workers who were also preparing the cellar of a new house. Another man unearthed six bodies while digging postholes for his barnyard and another while digging a well.

An article in the March 31, 1904 edition of the *Pittsfield Sun* mentioned an additional Mohican burial site farther north in the county, near Pittsfield, on the east side of the Housatonic River. The writer asserted that the Mohicans often made "pious pilgrimages" by canoe to that location. And he went on to mention yet another site along the river: "Some of their skeletons, too, have been exhumed from the eastern bank of its outlet from Lake Pontoosuc, where they had been interred in the usual sitting posture."

According to historian Shirley Dunn, another Mohican burial ground was uncovered in 1784 by workmen who were breaking ground for a new meetinghouse in Stockbridge. That town had been settled half a century before as a mission to the Mohicans in the region, and many of the town plots initially belonged to native landowners. But by the 1780s, most of those deeds were rescinded, and the few Mohicans who remained were forced to move west, ultimately ending up in Wisconsin as the Stockbridge-Munsee Nation. According to Lion Miles in "The Red Man Dispossessed," the last deed to be sold off by Mohican landowners was the site of this burial ground, which is located at the west end of Main Street beside the present-day Stockbridge Golf Club. The deed stipulated that the land was to be set aside and that the bones of the ancestors who lie there must never be disturbed. In 1877, this site was memorialized with a stone monument that remains there to this day.

THE GRAVES OF EARLY SETTLERS

Deacon John Jackson speaks from the grave: "As I am now, so you must be. Therefore, prepare to follow me." *Courtesy of Robert Oakes.*

According to an article by Abby Pratt in the October 29, 1992 issue of the *Berkshire Eagle*, the oldest grave of a white settler in the Berkshires is that of Matthew Noble, who came to the region from Westfield in 1725. Quoting Sheffield's then-cemetery commissioner Milton Barnum, Pratt described Noble's stone as small, modest and illegible. It was located beside his daughter's at the back of the Sheffield Plain Cemetery on South Main Street.

Also among the earliest graves of white settlers in the Berkshires is that of Reverend Adonijah Bidwell, the first minister of then-Housatonic Township Number One (today, it is the separate towns of Monterey and Tyringham). Bidwell, who was born in Hartford,

Connecticut, in 1716, was buried in 1784 in Woods Cemetery, which is located on a small hill beside Beartown Mountain Road in Monterey. Nearby are the graves of his first and second wives, Theodosia Colton and Jemima Devotion. Also nearby is the grave of John Jackson, the first deacon of the church, who was buried in 1757.

THE SEDGWICK PIE

Stockbridge Cemetery

Near the back of the Stockbridge Cemetery is a most unusual sight: nearly 150 stones set in concentric rings around an obelisk and an urn. Known as the Sedgwick Pie, this section of the cemetery is strictly reserved for the members of one of New England's most prominent families, the Sedgwicks. Patriarch Theodore (1746–1813)—known to the family as the Judge—was a prominent attorney, politician, justice of the Massachusetts Supreme Judicial Court, member of the first Congress and friend to George Washington. Theodore and his wife, Pamela, raised seven children,

The Sedgwick Pie, where members of a prominent New England family are buried in rings around their forebears. *Courtesy of Robert Oakes.*

establishing a long family line that has included such luminaries as writer Catharine Sedgwick, editor Ellery Sedgwick, actress and model Edie Sedgwick and actress Kyra Sedgwick.

An abolitionist and defender of human rights, Theodore was also noted for representing Elizabeth Freeman (Mumbet), an enslaved woman, when she filed one of the first "freedom suits" in Massachusetts. Freeman was swiftly granted her liberty and later came to work for the Sedgwick family, with whom she had grown very close—so close, in fact, that Freeman was also buried inside the family circle. It is said that each body in the pie is laid with its feet facing inward, toward Theodore and Pamela at the center, so that, on the day of the resurrection, while others will rise toward the sun in the east, the Sedgwicks will rise to greet their family forebears.

While the Sedgwick Pie is unusual, it is not unique in the Berkshires. A similar—though smaller—arrangement can be found in the Center Cemetery on Berkshire School Road in Sheffield, where thirteen members of the Spurr family are buried in a ring around a central obelisk.

THE BERKSHIRE BODY SNATCHERS

There was once a time when grave robbery was not uncommon in the Berkshires. As Bernard R. Carman wrote in the July 23, 1955 issue of the *Berkshire Eagle*, reports of body snatching in Berkshire County go back as far as 1754, when two Pittsfield men were arrested for "digging up and scalping an Indian which was buried" in an attempt to claim a bounty. "In Berkshire, there was hardly a village in which one or more graves had not been robbed," noted Pittsfield historian Joseph E.A. Smith in his 1887 book, *The History of Pittsfield, Massachusetts*. Smith went on to tell the story of Pittsfield police officer Timothy Hall, who "saw what appeared to be a white figure bowing to him" as he passed a graveyard. Not wanting to be marked a "ghost-coward for life, [Hall] approached the mysterious object" and discovered that it was a shroud that had been left behind by body snatchers. The disinterred body from which it had been torn had been dragged out of a broken coffin in the way that body snatchers typically procured their prey back then: they pulled the corpse from the coffin with an iron hook under its chin. Understandably, such an awful violation horrified the public and drove many to riot.

In Pittsfield, in 1820, tensions were high after it was discovered that the body of George Butler Jr. had been stolen from the town cemetery, which was located near the present-day common. Butler had died in November 1819, and during the winter that followed, his mother had had a recurring dream that her son's grave was empty. The following spring, another of her sons opened the grave to find that the body was indeed missing. Many were shocked. The grave was left open so that all could look into it and see the shattered, empty coffin. A town meeting was called to bring an end to the body stealing, but the committee soon realized that no laws forbidding the practice existed. The matter was brought before the governor, but a law was not passed to protect the dead until 1830. In the meantime, townspeople like Josiah Bissell, who owned a store near the town cemetery, had no choice but to keep a neighborhood watch over the graves. The people remained vigilant, and tensions remained high.

So, in 1822, when plans were proposed to build a new Berkshire Medical College beside the same cemetery from which Butler's body had so recently been stolen, townspeople were up in arms. In those days, many believed that medical school students regularly engaged in the grisly practice of body snatching. While there were legal ways for medical colleges to procure the bodies they needed for study, there were often not enough available, and particularly in rural areas, transportation

A grave robbery at the site of the present-day common horrified the public and drove many to riot. *Courtesy of Katherine Oakes.*

of cadavers was difficult. So, some medical students were suspected of resorting to "odious midnight prowlings." As mentioned in the October 12, 1917 edition of the *Berkshire Eagle*, "in those dark ages of medical research, body snatching was the rule."

The trustees of the proposed college sent out circulars that assured the public no such illegal body snatching would be tolerated at their institution. And while local graveyards did indeed seem to become safer after the school's construction, thefts were soon reported from graveyards further afield. When those were traced back to students at the Berkshire Medical College, some locals threatened to tear the college buildings down if the bodies were not returned. They were returned intact, and the students responsible were arrested. During the next town meeting, resolutions were passed to condemn the practice of body snatching. Laws that protected the dead while also making the bodies of paupers and criminals available for dissection followed soon after. Together, these new laws put an end to the rampant body snatching in the Berkshires and beyond.

THE CHURCH-ON-THE-HILL CEMETERY

Though fascinating, none of the graveyards previously mentioned are said to be haunted. However, there may be a spirit lingering in the Church-on-the-Hill Cemetery at the intersection of Main and Greenwood Streets in Lenox. Local blogger Kim Ostellino (www.berkshiregirlonline.com) mentions that the ghost of a prominent Lenox woman is said to haunt the site. The cemetery was set aside as a burying ground in 1770 and is now the final resting place for many former residents and notable figures, including Teddy Wharton, Annie Haggerty Shaw and Serge Koussevitzky. According to the Lenox History site, the earliest people laid to rest there were interred according to colonial custom, with their feet facing east so that they could rise to greet the dawn on Judgment Day. It is also likely that children played among the graves in those early days while their parents attended lengthy church services.

Famed Lenox resident, author and actress Fanny Kemble once said of the Church-on-the-Hill Cemetery, "I will not rise to trouble anyone if they will let me sleep here. I will ask only to be permitted, once in a while, to raise my head and look out on this glorious scene." However, it is not Kemble's spirit that is said to haunt the cemetery; rather, it is the spirit of Hannah Lydig, who

The ghost of a prominent Lenox woman may roam the graves in the Church-on-the-Hill Cemetery. *Courtesy of Robert Oakes.*

died in 1930 and was buried there alongside her husband, David. Ostellino wrote that some have seen her ghost "roaming through the gravestones or caught a picture of her in the church windows."

LITTLE GIRL LOST

The West Branch Road Cemetery

Perhaps the most notoriously haunted Berkshire graveyard is the West Branch Road Cemetery on October Mountain, which is said to be haunted by the ghost of ten-year-old Anna Pease, who was buried there on January 22, 1829. To find it, you have to drive into the woods along rocky, dirt roads, departing the paved highway that skirts the state forest through the town of Washington. To find it—for the first time—you have to believe it is there because no signs point the way, and the deeper you drive into the woods, the further you will feel from any place that has ever been inhabited by people. And as the dark woods surround you, you might remember the eerie stories you have heard about this mountain—stories of an unseen presence, of eyes peering through tree trunks, of sasquatch sightings and even of strange lights hovering overhead in the night. You might feel inclined, then, to turn back, but if you persist, you will be rewarded. The graveyard is there, though its stones are crumbling, and the forest is reclaiming it.

This cemetery has existed since the early 1800s, a time when hardy farmers and woodcutters had only recently established the earliest farms, mills and villages on the rocky heights. At that time, this location likely would have seemed less lonesome, closer to the bustle of daily life. But today, it is deep inside October Mountain State Park, a 16,500-acre nature preserve bordered by the towns of Washington, Becket, Lee and Lenox. People go there to enjoy hiking, boating, camping and fishing. They find a peaceful escape among its wooded roads and trails, but few stop to pay their respects to the dead who still lie in this quiet clearing—silent witnesses to the region's distant past.

There have been visitors through the years who have noted the effects of time on the cemetery—the loss of stones and the encroachment of the undergrowth. Some, like workers from the department of conservation and recreation, still help to preserve the cemetery by mowing and maintaining the grass. Paranormal investigators and ghost hunters come now and again to try to catch a glimpse of the ghost or to listen for voices or a mysterious humming sound that has been reported there. In 2014, New England legend hunter Jeff Belanger brought descendants of the Washington Peases to the site to lay flowers on Annie's grave. And in 2016, "bone finder" Robert Perry used radar and GPS devices to map the location of the site's fifty-five graves. He determined that many more lie beneath the ground than the number of remaining stones suggest and that some have been completely engulfed by the forest.

But after the visitors leave and the hikers move on, after the mowers and mapping devices are powered down and put away, the slow silence of centuries past returns. The sun slips down beneath the tree line; shafts of its golden light slide unhurriedly across the grass, letting a brief illumination fall on the broken headstones and the faded names of the ones who lie below: Emily S., wife of David Ingalls; Isaac Nelson Barnum; Cobb Codding; Lucinda Pease; and of course, little Anna Pease, aged ten years, nine months. Almost nothing seems to be known about Anna's life and death. According to genealogical records, Anna was born on May 14,

A ghostly girl dressed all in white is said to haunt the West Branch Road Cemetery on October Mountain. *Courtesy of Katherine Oakes.*

1818; she was the seventh of the ten children who were born to Oliver Pease, a farmer from Enfield, Connecticut, who had settled in Washington in 1804 and had married Katherine Chappell. Both Oliver and Katherine now lie buried beside their daughter's grave, along with the other members of the Pease family.

There is a feeling of deep calm here. You can sense the years that have passed and the presence of another world, another time and the lives lived long ago. There is also a feeling of sadness, an atmosphere of longing. Do these spirits want to see their stones set upright again? Do they feel neglected and lost out here, forgotten by the world? Do they just want us to remember them, to bring them home to our hearths and hearts through the stories that we share? Very little is left now aside from those memories, stones and stories, like the one people tell of a ghostly girl, dressed all in white, stepping lightly among the gravestones.

5.
THE GHOSTLY MUSE
AND SPIRITUAL SPIRITS

HIGHWOOD'S GHOST AT TANGLEWOOD

Can music connect us to the otherworld? Maybe that depends on what and where we play. At Tanglewood in Lenox, on any summer day, sweet sounds echo through the trees. Whether it's from students rehearsing or a symphony resounding, the grounds are alive with the sound of music. But if you listen closely, you may also hear a resident spirit on the wind, a spirit that, some say, is especially drawn to music and the maestros who make it.

Founded in 1937, Tanglewood is the summer home of the Boston Symphony Orchestra (BSO), which offers a series of concerts each season to hundreds of thousands of Berkshire music lovers. The venue's open-air halls, which are surrounded by green meadows and leafy woods, allow for a beautiful fusion of art and nature. Tanglewood is a significant cultural landmark that also features pop music concerts and educational programs. It has long been associated with musical legends like Leonard Bernstein, John Williams, James Taylor and Yo-Yo Ma. But the property's cultural roots go much deeper, extending into the soil of nineteenth-century transcendentalism, a movement of spiritually inclined writers and thinkers, including Ralph Waldo Emerson, Henry David Thoreau and Margaret Fuller, who sought to connect with the divine presence they sensed in nature. That movement also included a Boston banker and aspiring poet named Samuel Gray Ward, who, in 1844, purchased a portion of the farm that once occupied the property, with its little red farmhouse and views of the

Stockbridge Bowl. There, Ward and his wife, Anna, built Highwood, a three-story Gothic Revival home that is considered to be the first of the Berkshire cottages. The Wards invited friends and fellow transcendentalists William and Caroline Tappan to stay in the farmhouse, which the Tappans later purchased, along with a 210-acre parcel adjacent to the Wards' property.

When the Wards moved back to Boston so that Samuel could run the family banking business for his ailing father, the Tappans moved into Highwood and rented out the farmhouse to author Nathaniel Hawthorne, who was also affiliated with the transcendentalists. During his residence there, between 1850 and 1851, Hawthorne wrote one of his most significant works, *The House of Seven Gables*, as well as *The Wonder Book*, a collection of Greek myth adaptations. Famously, Hawthorne imagined the back porch of Highwood as the place where his fictional storyteller, Eustace Bright, regaled his young audience with tales of ancient heroes and monsters. In 1865, the Tappans built their own house, which they called Tanglewood in honor of Hawthorne, who had originally coined the name, inspired by the property's dense and sinuous trees.

More than seventy years later, in 1937, the Tappan family bequeathed the Tanglewood House and its grounds to the BSO, just in time to provide

Does a music-loving spirit haunt Highwood on the grounds of Tanglewood? *Courtesy of Robert Oakes.*

a home for the fledgling summer music festival. As for Highwood, several private families resided there until 1986, when the BSO bought it, effectively doubling the size of the music venue. It was around that time that word began to spread of the ghost of Highwood Manor. Staff and visitors alike reported blasts of hot and cold air, disembodied sighs, mysteriously running faucets, audible footsteps, lights switching on and off and doors opening and closing. One employee said she felt her hair being lifted from her shoulders by an unseen hand, and another heard the sound of someone moving around on the second floor, despite no one being up there at the time. In an article in the July 26, 1992 edition of the *Berkshire Eagle*, Andrew Pincus reported that patrons of a supper club that operated out of Highwood Manor refused to be seated on the second floor because they found the "atmosphere uncomfortable." Pincus also reported that supper club wait staff avoided the second floor and would run downstairs if they were ever left up there alone. Director Bill Cosel, who used the top floor of Highwood for an office during the summer of 1986, said he, too, felt a presence in the house. "There was a service corkscrew stairs that was a shortcut to our office," said Cosel. "Creepy ascension every time. It took me weeks to get up the nerve to go down the main grand staircase, with balustrades and high ceilings…plenty of room for floating spirits!"

Some at the time blamed the sudden awakening of paranormal activity on the disturbance of the tombstone of Oreb Andrews, a farm hand who was killed on the property in 1822 by a falling tree. According to reports, Tanglewood workmen moved the stone while clearing space for a parking lot, leading some to wonder whether the spirit of the long-dead farmhand was abroad at night, out to disturb his disturbers. Others believed that the activity increased after staff members hung photographs of Leonard Bernstein and other notable Tanglewood artists on the second floor. According to the article by Pincus, a parapsychologist who once investigated the house believed the spirit to be that of a child who was especially drawn to those with a sensitive, artistic nature.

Bernstein himself was said to have encountered the Highwood ghost on the infamous second floor. Between 1986 and his death in 1990, the celebrated composer and conductor used one of those rooms as an office. It was there, in 1990, just two months before he died, that he reportedly leapt from his seat, threw his hands up toward the ceiling and shouted, "What is it that's there? Who is it that's there?" BSO volunteer Barbara Greenbaum said, "Lenny really believed in ghosts. He really did!" She went on to describe a kind of musical séance that Bernstein arranged shortly

pacifism, political neutrality and a total devotion to God, but others were suspicious of these religious recluses and subjected them to imprisonment, forced removals, ridicule and accusations of moral depravity and dealings with the Devil. In spite of this, the Shakers have had a lasting impact on American society, and though very few remain alive today, the movement continues to inspire curiosity and fascination.

In recent years, some of this interest has focused on Shaker ghosts. In 2012, author Thomas Lee Freese published *Shaker Spirits, Shaker Ghosts*, a collection of stories about alleged encounters at the Shaker Village of Pleasant Hill in Kentucky and the White Water Shaker Village in Ohio. Around the same time, the Hancock Shaker Village living-history museum in the Berkshires began offering its "Haunted Hancock" tour, during which guides share tales of reported sightings as they walk the darkened grounds.

But this fascination with Shaker spirits began at least as far back as the 1980s. In his 1986 book, *Ghosts in Residence*, H.A. Von Behr wrote of the spirits that are said to haunt the old chair factory at the site of the Mount Lebanon Shaker community in New Lebanon, just over the New York border from Hancock. Von Behr wrote of owners Louise and Donald MacDonald and the hauntings they began to experience shortly after moving into the historic building—mostly in their third-floor bedroom, and always at 1:30 a.m. Donald described hearing footsteps on the stairs and in the halls and the sound of pounding, hammering and the turning of wheels. Then, one night, the couple woke to the rattle of a door latch—as if someone was trying to enter the room—followed by the apparition of a woman in a long black cape passing through the unopened door, moving along one wall and then passing again through the opposite door. On another night, Donald said the figure of a bearded man in Victorian-style clothing passed through the same door, sat down on the bed beside his wife, appeared to take her hand and then stood up and vanished. Von Behr pondered whether the old factory was haunted by the spirits of Shakers who resented the invasion of their once-Edenic religious community by worldly people. This chapter of *Ghosts in Residence* became the basis of a column in the November 14, 1986 issue of the *Berkshire Eagle* by Richard V. Happel, who wondered—as many ghost seekers still do today—whether "the Hancock Shaker community has ever been haunted by embittered Shakers past."

What Von Behr and Happel may not have known is that many of the Shakers' religious practices did indeed involve communing with the dead. Through spirit writing, mystical visions and visitations by angels and saints in dreams and trance-like dances, Shakers drew a great deal of guidance and inspiration from the spirit world. This began with founder, Mother Ann Lee, who, while living in England, claimed to receive messages from beyond, instructing her to establish her order in the New World. Once in America, Mother Ann and other elders continued to be guided by such revelations, known as "gifts."

These mysterious practices intensified during the period of Shaker history known as the Era of Manifestations, which began in the late 1830s, when several young women in Watervliet, New York, reportedly fell into a trance and awakened later to relay visions and messages transmitted to them by the spirits of Mother Ann and other long-dead elders of the order. Soon, this phenomenon began to spread throughout the Shaker communities, as other individuals, who came to be known as "inspired ones" or "instruments," began to report similar trance-like journeys into what they called "spirit land." According to reports, these instruments—most of them girls or young women—emerged from the trance speaking in the tongue of angels. Others returned with bits of poetry, prose and song that they claimed to hear while on the other side. Indeed, many well-known Shaker songs, like "Simple Gifts," were said to come through these inspired ones from spirit land.

Other instruments used visual art to depict the places, beings and objects they encountered in the other world. These evocative "gift drawings" contained images of trees, bowers, tables, crosses, faces, doves and holy crowns, often combined with comforting and encouraging messages transmitted through spirit writing from the angels, saints and ancestors. Some of these drawings also contained descriptions written by the artists themselves, who often seemed at a loss to describe their strange experience. "The bright-silver-color'd blaze streaming from the edges of each green leaf, resembles so many bright torches," wrote Hannah Cohoon in 1845. "I saw the whole tree as the angel held it before me as distinctly as I ever saw a natural tree. I felt very cautious when I took hold of it lest the blaze should touch my hand." On another tree drawing, Cohoon wrote that, when she asked Mother Ann to tell her the name of the tree, the spirit answered her, "by moving the hand of a medium to write twice over 'Your Tree is the Tree of Life.'"

During these years of spiritual rebirth and tremendous creative output, when inspired instruments produced thousands of songs and drawings, Shaker communities throughout the country also began establishing sacred gathering sites outside their villages, often on nearby mountaintops. Each contained a sacred altar stone, as well as a fountain described at the time as "not of literal waters, but of the water of life." Around it, the devotees would whirl and dance and fall under trances, and it is said that thousands of spirits and angels would descend on them from the heavens. After hours

At the top of Shaker Mountain, it is said that thousands of spirits would descend on devotees from above. *Courtesy of Robert Oakes.*

of frenzied dancing, instruments were known to faint and then rise up again, speaking in tongues.

While these mountaintop gatherings awed some contemporary observers, others mocked them and even suspected satanic ritual. In her 2017 *Travel + Leisure* piece "Driving New England Shaker Settlement," Rachel Urquhart, the author of the Shaker-inspired novel *The Visionist*, referred to the many "rumors and half-truths" she heard as a child living in a former Shaker site in Tyringham. "Local farmers, suspicious of the Shakers and their strange ways, used to call the ceremonial site in the woods above the Tyringham settlement the Devil's Playground," she wrote. "Bizarre rites, drunkenness, and debauchery were said to have taken place up there." Pamphlets, too, were distributed, accusing the Shakers of all manner of crimes and sin.

Given these local superstitions, it isn't hard to understand how stories might have emerged, linking these mountaintop rites with the Evil One. One such story, written in 1934 by Willard Douglas Coxey in *Ghosts of Old Berkshire* as "The Devil Battle of Mt. Sinai," tells of how the Shakers captured and killed the Devil at the summit of the sacred mountain. Armed with a Bible and an invisible sword, the spirit warriors in Coxey's tale formed a ring around the base of the mountain and slowly ascended in an ever-tightening circle, singing hymns of faith. As they advanced, they saw no visible sign of the Devil but could smell the noxious smell of sulfur and hear "curses, mingled with hisses, as from a thousand venomous snakes." At last, "as the swords crossed in the heart of the circle, there was one long cry of hatred and baffled anger. Then silence." Satan was dead. The victorious warriors buried the Devil in a grave "piled high with boulders," then descended to the village to celebrate.

A similar story appeared in *A Hinterland Settlement: Tyringham, Massachusetts and Bordering Lands* by Eloise Myers. In this story, the Shakers of Tyringham were said to have "[driven the Devil] to the highest hill back of their village, Mount Horeb. [There], they buried him, face down, with clam shells in his hands, so that if he dug, he would go deeper instead of digging out." While in both of these stories the Shakers are, at least, seen to oppose rather than worship the Devil, such tales reduce what appears to have been profoundly inspired mystical experiences to the usual moralistic struggle of good against evil.

Others at the time seemed to dismiss the Shakers and their strange ways altogether. In her 1849 article "Magnetism among the Shakers," Catharine Sedgwick described an unexpected visit from an elderly member of the order, whom she described as "childlike and simple, content in conscious mediocrity." Though Sedgwick did allow that the Shakers may have had enough "truth or holiness…to light a dusky path to heaven," she referred to what may have been a common opinion at the time by observing, "They have a perfect conviction that they have dived to the bottom of the well and found the pearl of truth, while all the rest of the world look upon them as at the bottom of a well indeed, but without the pearl." This article contains some fascinating contemporary descriptions of the mountaintop dances and visionary gifts, as well as an eerie account of an exchange of an invisible white pear between a young man and a woman who was said to be famous for her spiritual gifts. Though the elderly Shaker who visited Sedgwick that night is depicted as sincere in his belief in the spiritual significance of this strange psychic exchange, Sedgwick suggests that the whole thing was nothing more than "some clandestine intercourse" between two young lovers who were forced to keep their tryst a secret, owing to the order's rule of celibacy. The "poor, childlike old man," Sedgwick implied, was just too simpleminded to detect the ruse.

By the end of the 1850s, the Shakers had dismantled their holy sites, destroyed the sacred altar stones and turned their focus, once again, to the work of farm and factory—"Hands to work, hearts to God," as Mother Ann once advised. Though the mountaintop dances stopped and the spirit visions vanished, their impact on the Shaker community—and on American culture as a whole—continued to resonate and was felt as recently as 2009, when Yo-Yo Ma, Itzhak Perlman, Anthony McGill and Gabriela Montero performed John Williams's arrangement of "Simple Gifts" to commemorate the inauguration of President Barack Obama. An entire nation listened with reverence that day to the simple melody at the core of that complex arrangement, a simple melody that may have come to us as a gift from spirit through a cloistered Shaker instrument in a trance-like vision.

Courtesy of Katherine Oakes.

AFTERWORD

I hope you have enjoyed this exploration of the history and mysteries of these beautiful Berkshire Hills as much as I enjoyed researching and writing about them. And now, I hope that you will put this book down, walk out into the woods or through the rooms of an old house and peer into the shadows beyond the beam of your flashlight. And I hope that, when you do, you will be inspired to tell stories of your own. Lore is a living thing; we need to feed it to keep it alive, and each one of us has something to contribute. So, I hope you will reach out into the darkness with your senses open and your imagination engaged. And I hope you make contact with a mysterious presence that awakens your sense of wonder.

BIBLIOGRAPHY

Books

Abbott, Katharine M. *Old Paths and Legends of New England: Saunterings Over Historic Roads with Glimpses of Picturesque Fields and Old Homesteads in Massachusetts, Rhode Island, and New Hampshire.* New York: G.P. Putnam's Sons, 1904.

Belanger, Jeff, et al. *Weird Massachusetts: Your Travel Guide to Massachusetts's Local Legends and Best Kept Secrets.* New York: Sterling Publishing, 2008.

Bernard, Ronald, and Bernard A. Drew. *Sandisfield Then and Now: 1762–2012.* Sandisfield, MA: Town of Sandisfield 250th Anniversary Committee, 2012.

Blum, Deborah. *Ghost Hunters: William James and the Search for Scientific Proof of Life after Death.* New York: Penguin Books, 2007.

Bryan, Clark W. *Book of Berkshire: Describing and Illustrating Its Hills and Homes and Telling Where They Are.* Great Barrington and Springfield, MA: Hardpress Ltd., 1886.

Citro, Joseph A. *Passing Strange: True Tales of New England Hauntings and Horrors.* Boston: Houghton Mifflin, 1997.

———. *Weird New England: Your Travel Guide to New England's Local Legends and Best Kept Secrets.* New York: Sterling Publishing, 2005.

Collier, Edward Augustus. *A History of Old Kinderhook: From Aboriginal Days to the Present Time; Including the Story of the Early Settlers, Their Homesteads, Their Traditions, and Their Descendants.* New York: Putnam, 1914.

Coxey, Willard Douglas. *Ghosts of Old Berkshire.* Great Barrington, MA: Berkshire Courier, 1934.

Cushing, Thomas. *History of Berkshire County, Massachusetts: With Biographical Sketches of Its Prominent Men*. Farmington Hills, MI: Gale, 1885.

D'Agostino, Thomas. *A Guide to Haunted New England: Tales from Mount Washington to the Newport Cliffs*. Charleston, SC: The History Press, 2009.

De Tytus, Robb P., and Charles Cornell Van Siclen. *A Preliminary Report on the Re-Excavation of the Palace of Amenhetep III*. New York: Winthrop Press, 1903.

Drew, Bernard A. *Henry Knox and the Revolutionary War Trail in Western Massachusetts*. Jefferson, NC: McFarland & Company Inc., 2012.

Dunn, Shirley W. *The Mohican World, 1680–1750*. Fleischmanns, NY: Purple Mountain Press, 2000.

———. *The Mohicans and Their Land, 1609–1730*. Fleischmanns, NY: Purple Mountain Press, 1994.

Elliot, Louise E. *1777–1977, Two Hundred Years: The History of the Town of Washington, Massachusetts*. Washington, MA: Washington Historical Commission, 1977.

Fabian, Ann. *The Skull Collectors Race, Science, and America's Unburied Dead*. Chicago: University of Chicago Press, 2010.

Frazier, Patrick. *The Mohicans of Stockbridge*. Lincoln: University of Nebraska Press, 1992.

Freese, Thomas Lee. *Shaker Spirits, Shaker Ghosts*. Atglen, PA: Schiffer Publishing Ltd., 2012.

Garnett, Edna Bailey. *West Stockbridge, Massachusetts, 1774–1974: The History of an Indian Settlement, Queensborough or Qua-Pau-Kuk*. Berkshire, MA: *Berkshire Courier*, 1976.

Gilder, Cornelia Brooke. *Edith Wharton's Lenox*. Charleston, SC: The History Press, 2017.

Gilder, Cornelia Brooke, and Joan R. Olshansky. *A History of Ventfort Hall*. Lenox, MA: Ventfort Hall Association, 2002.

Gilder, Cornelia Brooke, and Julia Conklin Peters. *Hawthorne's Lenox: The Tanglewood Circle*. Charleston, SC: The History Press, 2008.

Goudsward, David. *Ancient Stone Sites of New England and the Debate Over Early European Exploration*. Jefferson, NC: McFarland & Co., 2006.

Greylock, Godfrey. *Taghconic, Or, Letters and Legends About Our Summer Home*. Ann Arbor, MI: University Microfilms International, 1879.

———. *Taghconic: The Romance and Beauty of the Hills*. Boston: Lee & Shepard, 1879.

Happel, Richard V., et al. *Berkshire, the First Three Hundred Years, 1676–1976*. Washington, D.C.: Eagle Publishing, 1976.

Harmon, Charlie. *On the Road and Off the Record with Leonard Bernstein: My Years with the Exasperating Genius*. Bournemouth, UK: Imagine!, 2018.

Hart, John S. *The Female Prose Writers of America: With Portraits, Biographical Notices, and Specimens of Their Writing*. Buffalo, NY: E.H. Butler, 1870.

Hauck, Dennis William. *Haunted Places: The National Directory, Ghostly Abodes, Sacred Sites, UFO Landings, and Other Supernatural Locations*. New York: Penguin Books, 2002.

Hawthorne, Nathaniel. *Tanglewood Tales*. London: Hesperus Minor, 2015.

Holzer, Hans. *Yankee Ghosts: Spine-Tingling Encounters with the Phantoms of New York and New England*. Dublin, NH: Yankee Books, 1966.

Hopkins, Samuel. *Historical Memoirs Relating to the Housatonic Indians*. Reprinted. New York: W. Abbatt, 1911.

Horjus, Maren. *Haunted Hikes: Real Life Stories of Paranormal Activity in the Woods*. London: Falcon Books Publishing, 2017.

Hunt, Thomas, et al. *A History of the County of Berkshire, Massachusetts in Two Parts: The First Being a General View of the County, the Second, an Account of the Several Towns*. Pittsfield, MA: Samuel W. Bush, 1829.

Jackson, Richard S., and Cornelia Brooke. *Houses of the Berkshires, 1870–1930*. New York: Acanthus Press, 2011.

Koomler, Sharon Duane. *Seen and Received: The Shakers' Private Art*. Pittsfield, MA: Hancock Shaker Village, 2000.

Kupperman, Karen Ordahl. *Indians and English: Facing Off in Early America*. Ithaca, NY: Cornell University Press, 2000.

Lake, Andrew. *Ghosthunting Southern New England*. Covington, KY: Clerisy Press, 2011.

Lewis, R.W.B. *Edith Wharton: A Biography*. New York: Vintage Books, 1993.

Loskiel, George Henry, and Christian Ignatius Latrobe. *History of the Mission of the United Brethren Among the Indians in North America*. London: Brethren's Society for the Furtherance of the Gospel, 1794.

Mavor, James W., and Byron E. Dix. *Manitou: The Sacred Landscape of New England's Native Civilization*. Rochester, VT: Inner Traditions International, 1989.

Myers, Arthur. *The Ghostly Register: Haunted Dwellings, Active Spirits: A Journey to America's Strangest Landmarks*. Chicago: Contemporary Books, 1986.

Myers, Eloise, and Clinton Elliott. *Tyringham: A Hinterland Settlement*. Tyringham, MA: Tyringham Historical Commission, 1989.

Newman, Rich. *The Ghost Hunters Field Guide*. Woodbury, MN: Llewellyn Publications, 2011.

Niles, Grace Greylock. *The Hoosac Valley: Its Legends and Its History*. New York: G.P. Putnam's Sons, 1912.

Owens, Carole. *The Berkshire Cottages: A Vanishing Era*. Round Hill, VA: Cottage Press, 1984.

———. *The Berkshires: Coach Inns to Cottages*. Charleston, SC: Arcadia Publishing, 2004.

Parrish, Lila S. *A History of Searles Castle in Great Barrington, Massachusetts: The Great Wigwam*. Great Barrington, MA: Attic Revivals Press, 1985.

Pitkin, David J. *Ghosts of the Northeast*. Torrance, CA: Aurora Publications, 2002.

Raby, David. *Walking Amongst the Shadows: Houghton Mansion*. Columbia, SC: self-published, 2018.

Revai, Cheri. *Haunted Massachusetts: Ghosts and Strange Phenomena of the Bay State*. Mechanicsburg, PA: Stackpole Books, 2005.

Rooney, E. Ashley, and D. Peter Lund. *Berkshire Ghosts, Legends, and Lore*. Atglen, PA: Schiffer Publishing, 2008.

Schlosser, S.E., and Paul G. Hoffman. *Spooky Massachusetts: Tales of Hauntings, Strange Happenings, and Other Local Lore*. Guilford, CT: Globe Pequot Press, 2008.

Shaw, Robert Gould, and Russell Duncan. *Blue-Eyed Child of Fortune: The Civil War Letters of Colonel Robert Gould Shaw*. Athens: University of Georgia Press, 1992.

Skinner, Charles M. *Myths and Legends of Our Own Land*. Philadelphia: J.B. Lippincott Co., 1896.

Smith, J.E.A. *The History of Pittsfield, (Berkshire County), Massachusetts, Comp. and Written, Under the General Direction of a Committee*. Springfield, MA: C.W. Bryan, 1869.

Smitten, Susan. *Ghost Stories of New England*. Edmonton, AB, Canada: Ghost House Books, 2003.

Spear, Willis F. *History of North Adams, Mass.: 1749–1885. Reminiscences of Early Settlers. Extracts Rom Old Town Records. Its Public Institution, Industries and Prominent Citizens, Together with a Roster of Commissioned Officers in the War of the Rebellion*. Eugene, OR: Clearwater Publishers, 1885.

Steiger, Brad. *Real Ghosts, Restless Spirits, and Haunted Places*. Canton, MI: Visible Ink Press, 2013.

Taylor, Charles James. *History of Great Barrington, (Berkshire County) Massachusetts*. Berwyn Heights, MD: Heritage Books, 1882.

Thompson, Dave. *Haunted America FAQ: All That's Left to Know about the Most Haunted Houses, Cemeteries, Battlefields, and More*. Milwaukee, WI: Hal Leonard Corporation, 2015.

Von Behr, H.A. *Ghosts in Residence*. Utica, NY: North Country Books, 1986.

Wallace, Paul A.W. *Indians in Pennsylvania*. Harrisburg, PA: Pennsylvania Historical and Museum Commission, 1961.

Warner, Charles F. *Picturesque Berkshire: Complete in Two Parts, with 1,200 Illustrations*. Northampton, MA: Picturesque Publishing Company, 1893.

Webb-Peploe, Annie. *Pilgrims of New England: A Tale of the Early American Settlers*. London: Simpkin, Marshall and Co., 1853.

Wharton, Edith. *Edith Wharton: Novellas and Other Writings*. New York: Library of America, 1990.

Newspaper, Journal, and Magazine Articles

Andrews, Edward D. "Ann Lee: From the Forge of Tragedy, a Leader." *Berkshire Eagle*, September 28, 1960.

———. "The Dawn of an Era and a Nation." *Berkshire Eagle*, September 26, 1960.

———. "Hancock: Last Chance to Preserve a Culture." *Berkshire Eagle*, October 1, 1960.

———. "Inventive Suppliers to the World They Shunned." *Berkshire Eagle*, September 30, 1960.

———. "Out of Persecution, Strength." *Berkshire Eagle*, September 27, 1960.

Bahlman, D.R. "Famous Personalities at the New Boston Inn." *Berkshire Eagle*, March 29, 2005.

Barlow, Steve. "Becket Quarry Beckons Hikers." *Berkshire Eagle*, May 20, 2005.

Bass, Milton. "Ashintully: The Music Is in the Landscape." *Berkshire Eagle*, July 5, 2001.

———. "The Changing Scene: The Haunting of Highwood." *Berkshire Eagle*, August 7, 1992.

———. "New Boston Inn: Old Stage Stop Offers French Cuisine." *Berkshire Eagle*, June 25, 1966.

———. "Resting Content in the Sedgwick Pie." *Berkshire Eagle*, June 18, 1989.

Beckwith, Robert H. "Our Indian Predecessors." *Berkshire Eagle*, February 15, 1963.

Bellow, Daniel O. "The Last Word: Ghostbuster." *Berkshire Eagle*, August 28, 1992.

Berkshire Eagle. "Accident Victim's Condition Serious." August 10, 1914.

———. "Among Famous Visitors to the Berkshires." October 22, 1964.

———. "Annual Quarry Celebration Day Includes Debut of New Historic Quarry Walk." August 25, 2005.

———. "Ashintully Mansion Razed by Tyringham Forest Fire." April 23, 1952.

———. "Ashintully, 35-Room Tyringham Landmark, Looks for Buyer." June 11, 1949.

———. "Auto Parties Had Very Narrow Escapes." May 21, 1917.

———. "Balance Rock Put in Its Present Precarious Position by Atotaroh's Duff." January 19, 1929.

———. "Barrington School Is Sold for $100,000 to J.J. Joyce." September 27, 1950.

———. "Bash Bish." December 29, 1892.

———. "Bash Bish Falls." July 10, 1908.

———. "Bash Bish Falls." June 20, 1931.

———. "Bash Bish Falls." August 16, 1991.

———. "Bash Bish Inn Owner Arrested." November 25, 1911.

———. "Becket Land Trust Historic Quarry and Forest: Quarry Celebration Day." August 24, 2006.

———. "Berkshire County Historical Timeline." September 5, 1894.

———. "Boston Publisher Seriously Hurt." July 26, 1911.

———. "Bucksteep Manor Is Sold: Family Center Is Planned." October 5, 1971.

———. "Bucksteep Manor to Be Opened Saturday." June 21, 1934.

———. "Charles D. Strickland Obituary." October 5, 1961.

———. "Chauffeur of the Fatal Car Commits Suicide." August 3, 1914.

———. "Chester and Becket Line Abandoned." April 24, 1931.

———. "Chicago Couple Planning to Buy New Boston Inn." November 24, 1984.

———. "City Mourns Death of Ex-Mayor Houghton." August 13, 1914.

———. "Death Comes to Mrs. Clapp After Long Illness." February 20, 1908.

———. "Death of Thaddeus Clapp." November 6, 1890.

———. "Fell 20 Feet." June 20, 1907.

———. "Fire at Bash Bish Inn." August 31, 1918.

———. "Former Mayor Fourth Victim of Auto Crash." August 12, 1914.

———. "Funeral of Rev. Dr. Davis to Be Held on Monday." August 26, 1910.

———. "Funerals of Victims of Auto Accident." August 4, 1914.

———. "General Knox Marker in Otis Is Dedicated Today." June 30, 1928.

————. "The Ghost of Mallery Hill Still Guards 'Haunted House.'" July 9, 1955.

————. "Hearing Tomorrow on Future Concerts at Bucksteep Manor." June 17, 1981.

————. "The Indians of Berkshire." April 1, 1904.

————. "Its Name Ashintully: The New Tytus Estate in Tyringham—The Occupants." August 13, 1908.

————. "Jennie J. Clark Obituary." March 15, 1993.

————. "Lack of Snow Bedevils Region." January 15, 1989.

————. "Lady Mary's Castle." July 7, 1962.

————. "Letter Recalls Days When Body Snatching Prevailed." October 12, 1917.

————. "Letter to the Editor: Ashintully by Norman Dellert." April 28, 1952.

————. "Made Trip on Bash Bish Road." December 8, 1914.

————. "Marriage and Loss of Wife." September 14, 1855.

————. "A Matter of Locomotion: How the Chester and Becket Railroad Is Conducted." July 12, 1899.

————. "New Boston Inn Leased." March 16, 1946.

————. "New Boston Inn Sold for $25,000 to Barnstable Mother, Daughter." October 7, 1964.

————. "Newton Concern Plans to Acquire Tyringham Estate." February 9, 1937.

————. "Night Spot at Seven Hills Resort Is Open to the Berkshire Public." July 13, 1985.

————. "Offered Use of Estate for Season." May 28, 1925.

————. "One Killed and Four Injured, Auto Goes Over Embankment." August 1, 1914.

————. "Outdoor Activities Calendar." June 3, 2005.

————. "A Palace Wonder: Searles Mansion to be a Conservatory for Study of the Organ." October 27, 1897.

————. "Paranormal Conference to Be Held." September 21, 2006.

————. "Phantoms of Shoon-keek and Moon-keek Still Haunt Quiet Waters of Pontoosuc Lake." January 12, 1929.

————. "Pontoosuc Woolen Co. Is a Family Concern: In Business a Century." May 12, 1928.

————. "Pontoosuc Woolen Company Sold to New York Concern after Century of Business." August 14, 1928.

————. "Professor's Wife Falls to Death at Bash Bish Falls, in Taconic Park." June 28, 1930.

————. "Program to Discuss Searles Castle." September 27, 2004.

————. "Rev. Dr. W.V.W. Davis Instantly Killed by Fall Over Ledge of Rocks." August 25, 1910.

————. "Saco Plans Resort for 'Singles' at Bucksteep Manor in Washington." April 22, 1972.

————. "Shaker Colony Property Sold for $125,000." December 10, 1960.

————. "Sheffield's 13 Cemeteries by Abby Pratt." October 29, 1992.

————. "600 Attend Bucksteep Manor Powwow." September 17, 1979.

————. "Skull Crushed Against Big Boulder." August 27, 1917.

————. "Sleeping with Ghosts: Local B&Bs Offer 'Spirited' Experiences." September 2, 2004.

————. "Spirit of Highwood Captures Imaginations." July 30, 1992.

————. "Tenth Bucksteep Anniversary to Be Observed." July 6, 1946.

————. "Thespian's Theatricals." February 13, 1890.

————. "Tragedy in Lenox." March 10, 1956.

————. "Travel Channel to Feature Haunted Hotel in Lenox." October 29, 2003.

————. "Tri-State Park Would Include Bash Bish in the Berkshire Country." November 6, 1922.

————. "Virginia K. Strong Obituary." October 17, 1981.

————. "Washington Residents Grieved by the Recent Death of George Crane." October 7, 1933.

————. "Wild Deer Damage Crops in Central Berkshire." December 28, 1904.

————. "Youth Conference Is Third This Season for Episcopal Center, Bucksteep Manor." July 29, 1939.

Boston Globe. "A.C. Houghton Dead." August 12, 1914.

————. "Berkshire's Palace Wonder." October 17, 1897.

————. "Egyptian Cosmetic Jar Reposes in a Villa in the Berkshire Hills." April 20, 1924.

————. "4 Jesuits Die in Fire." March 10, 1956.

————. "Jewels Valued at $150,000 Stolen: Home of Mrs. J.S. McLennan, Tyringham, Entered." October 3, 1918.

————. "Kept on the Go: President KcKinley Puts in Busy Day." September 26, 1897.

————. "Like Windsor Castle Is Kellogg Terrace at Great Barrington." May 10, 1891.

————. "Mrs. Hartman Kuhn Dead." October 7, 1908.

————. "One Killed at No. Pownal, VT." August 1, 1914.

———. "Rev. Dr. Davis Breaks Neck: Falls Over Ledge at Bash Bish Falls." August 26, 1910.

———. "Scent on Roehl and Pallister." April 28, 1893.

———. "The Vampires of Berkshire." December 27, 1908.

———. "Whitney's Lodge Looted." October 10, 1908.

———. "The World Walled Out." September 23, 1890.

Brooklyn Daily Eagle. "Berkshires." July 29, 1900.

Brown, Henry, et al. "As It Appears that Some Interest Has Been Excited…" *Pittsfield Sun,* July 27, 1837.

Brown, Seth. "Enter the Twilight Zone." *Berkshire Eagle,* October 30, 2008.

Browne, William B. "Over Pathways of the Past." *North Adams Transcript,* November 11, 1940.

Bulkeley, Morgan. "Bash Bish." *Berkshire Eagle,* August 5, 1961.

———. "Our Berkshires: Requiem for a Lake." *Berkshire Eagle,* March 19, 1970.

———. "Our Berkshires: Will Bash Bish Be Damned?" *Berkshire Eagle,* December 1, 1966.

Carman, Bernard R. "Bygone Berkshire: Ghouls of the Medical School." *Berkshire Eagle,* July 23, 1955.

Carnes, Maryann. "Historian at Work: New Ashford Man Digs into Cemetery Records." *Berkshire Eagle,* February 28, 1993.

Cebula, Timothy Q. "Couple Reopen New Boston Inn." *Berkshire Eagle,* March 12, 2000.

Chapman, Dorothy W. "Bucksteep Manor Barn Converted into Nightspot, Ski-Touring Center." *Berkshire Eagle,* January 13, 1979.

———. "Outdoor Concerts Draw Scattered Complaints." *Berkshire Eagle,* June 19, 1981.

Chapman, Gerard. "Our Berkshires: William C. Whitney." *Berkshire Eagle,* June 9, 1987.

Cherryvale Republican. "Freakish Searles." August 3, 1899.

Chicago Tribune. "Mrs. Mark Hopkins Dead." July 26, 1891.

De La Mater, Benning W. "Graveyards Quiet but Fraught with Fright." *Berkshire Eagle,* October 31, 2005.

Deming, Francis. "Once Upon a Midnight Dreary: The Ghost of the New Boston Inn." *Sandisfield Times,* October 2011.

Deming, Nathaniel, et al. "To the Public." *Pittsfield Sun,* August 25, 1825.

Dew, Jack. "Eerie Inn in Lenox." *Berkshire Eagle,* May 18, 2003.

Drew, Bernard A. "Our Berkshires: Last Wooden Derrick." *Berkshire Eagle,* August 26, 2006.

Duby, Cindy. "Trust Outlines Plans for Becket Quarry Site." *Berkshire Eagle*, January 22, 2000.

Edwards, Janet M. "Source of the Legend." *Berkshire Eagle*, April 23, 1962.

Esch, Mary. "Area Waterfalls Abound." *Berkshire Eagle*, September 23, 2007.

———. "Author and Guide Tells Tales of Hundreds of Waterfalls. *Daily Intelligencer*, November 4, 2007.

Fanto, Clarence. "Mount Washington." *Berkshire Eagle*, April 24, 2007.

Fitchburg Sentinel. "Good Hiding Place Believed to Have Been Found by Escaped Murders at Mt. Washington, Mass." April 28, 1893.

———. "Washington: Town Has Few Conveniences but Plenty of Beauty." *Berkshire Eagle*, July 24, 2007.

Gallant, Betty. "Bucksteep Manor to Become Tutorial Camp for Children." *Berkshire Eagle*, March 26, 1966.

Gentile, Derek. "New Life at the Old Inn." *Berkshire Eagle*, November 12, 1988.

———. "Reward Offered for Statue Taken from Family Gravesite." *Berkshire Eagle*, September 4, 2003.

———. "T'was a Dark and Stormy Night: Eerie Stories Aplenty in County." *Berkshire Eagle*, October 27, 1996.

Gettysburg Times. "Carnegie Lies in Sleepy Hollow." August 14, 1919.

Gosselin, Lisa. "Innkeepers Will Restore Mansion on Wendell Ave." *Berkshire Eagle*, February 17, 2002.

Happel, Richard V. "Notes and Footnotes." *Berkshire Eagle*, November 14, 1986.

———. "Notes and Footnotes: Smoke Rings." *Berkshire Eagle*, January 27, 1967.

Hartford Courant. "Notes from Sage's Ravine and Bash Bish." September 28, 1854.

Hatch, Bishop. "Plans for Bucksteep Manor Confirmed." *Berkshire Eagle*, May 23, 1966.

Houston Chronicle. "Ghost Reports Rattle Music Fest." July 31, 1992.

Indianapolis Journal. "Mr. Whitney's Estate." October 12, 1902.

Kahn, Joseph P. "Names and Faces: Tanglewood Phantom." *Boston Globe*, July 30, 1992.

Knox, John B. "Berkshire Era Fades with Years." *Rhinelander Daily News*, June 20, 1951.

———. "Berkshire Luxury-Palace Era Fades with the Passing Years." *Escanaba Daily Press*, June 28, 1951.

Lehmann, Isabella. "Pontoosuc Legend." *Berkshire Eagle*, April 20, 1962.

McCarthy, Frank V. "Shadowbrook Burns—4 Die." *Berkshire Eagle*, March 10, 1956.

Michaels, Julie. "Tanglewood Area Balks at a Prison." *New York Times*, February 27, 1977.

Miles, Lion G. "The Red Man Dispossessed: The Williams Family and the Alienation of Indian Land in Stockbridge, Massachusetts, 1736–1818." *New England Quarterly* 67, no. 1 (1994): 46.

Minneapolis Journal. "A New Lodge of Elks in New York." November 3, 1903.

Minneapolis Sunday Tribune. "Haymakers Find Old Mummy." July 23, 1911.

Miyazawa, Yuki. "'Because He's Not Here': Edith Wharton's Study in the Afterlife, Ghosts, and the Art of Belief." *Edith Wharton Review* 34, no. 1 (2018): 47.

Morning News. "Death of Mrs. Searles." July 27, 1891.

Moore, Steve. "Historic New Boston Inn Scheduled for Reopening." *Berkshire Eagle*, April 20, 1991.

Morton, Thomas O., Jr. "Red Feather House Welcomes Public Tomorrow." *Berkshire Eagle*, June 4, 1955.

Mulvaney, Jay. "Reinventing the Bed and Breakfast." *Berkshire Eagle*, May 23, 2002.

Myers, Arthur B. "Nobody Home in the Dens of the Timber Rattlers." *Berkshire Eagle*, June 18, 1957.

New York Sun. "A.P. Stokes Badly Hurt." August 13, 1899.

New York Times. "A.P. Stokes Is Dead at His City Home." June 29, 1913.

———. "Autumn Gayeties in Lenox." September 17, 1893.

———. "Four Jesuits Die in Seminary Fire." March 11, 1956.

———. "Picture 'Talked' to Henry Adams." February 14, 1937.

———. "Robb de Peyster Tytus: Former Member of Massachusetts House Dies at Saranac Lake." August 16, 1913.

———. "Stokes Abandons Shadow Brook Farm." April 28, 1903.

New York Tribune. "Cottagers Making Ready for Fall Season—Hotels Filled." August 24, 1902.

North Adams Transcript. "A.C. Houghton Very Low This Afternoon." August 8, 1914.

———. "Albert C. Houghton, City's Leading Citizen, Dies at Home at 3 O'Clock This Afternoon." August 11, 1914.

———. "Ashintully Back in Tytus Family: Tyringham Estate Recaptured to Save Ancient Forest." August 28, 1937.

———. "Bought Mount Washington Property." January 15, 1901.

———. "Break Whitney House on October Mountain." October 10, 1908.

————. "City Mourns Death of Leading Citizen." August 12, 1914.

————. "City's Activities Cease as a Final Tribute to A.C. Houghton's Memory." August 13, 1914.

————. "Death Claims Mrs. Houghton." February 26, 1918.

————. "Does 'Old Coot's' Ghost Still Haunt Mt. Greylock Slopes?" February 8, 1965.

————. "Ghost of Thunderbolt Photographed." January 27, 1939.

————. "Ghost on the Thunderbolt." January 19, 1939.

————. "Granted Divorce in Halifax, N.S., Court: Tyringham Woman Gets Decree and Alimony." August 29, 1927.

————. "Houghton Funeral." March 1, 1918.

————. "Houghton Residence Will Become Masonic Temple." August 2, 1927.

————. "Local Episcopal Quartet Off to Bucksteep Manor." July 13, 1942.

————. "Long-Smouldering Fire Damages Masonic Temple." April 20, 1960.

————. "Masonic Temple Work Progresses." August 16, 1928.

————. "Miss Houghton and Mrs. Hutton Both Lose Lives." August 1, 1914.

————. "New Boston Inn Changes Hands." October 9, 1964.

————. "New Masonic Temple Is Fruit of Long Effort." April 6, 1929.

————. "187th Anniversary of Successful Attack on Fort." August 21, 1933.

————. "Open Ashintully to Public's View: Benefit at Famous Tyringham Estate." August 12, 1940.

————. "Pittsfield Minister Falls Over Ledge to Death." August 25, 1910.

————. "Realty Men Get County Showplace: Ashintully, With Fine Marble Manor House in Tyringham, Is Exchanged." February 9, 1937.

————. "Replica of Fort Massachusetts Is Formally Dedicated." August 21, 1933.

————. "Scenes in Connection with Houghton Funeral." August 14, 1914.

————. "Takes His Life as Result of Fatal Auto Accident." August 3, 1914.

————. "The Widders Funeral." August 5, 1914.

————. "Widders' Life History Is Told in Affidavits." September 25, 1914.

————. "Will Buy the Site: The Fort Massachusetts Historical Society Formed Last Saturday Night." January 20, 1896.

Palme, Arthur. "Our Berkshires: Bash Bish." *Berkshire Eagle*, May 13, 1940.

Pincus, Andrew L. "The Ghost of Highwood." *Berkshire Eagle*, July 26, 1992.

————. "Ringing Out the Year of the Ghost." *Berkshire Eagle*, January 3, 1993.

Pittsfield Sun. "Bash Bish Falls: Journey of a Day." October 17, 1844.

———. "Berkshire Hills." October 21, 1886.

———. "Berkshire Scenery." July 10, 1890.

———. "Excursion to Bash Bish." July 21, 1887.

———. "A Few Days Since There Fell into Our Hands a Pamphlet…" July 4, 1833.

———. "The Indians of Berkshire." March 31, 1904.

Ragusa, Thomas A. "Great Road Marked for Future." *Berkshire Eagle*, November 19, 2009.

Rheaume, Patrick. "Take a Hike: The Becket Quarry Museum Offers a Unique Look at Local History." *Berkshire Eagle*, July 10, 2003.

Rud, A.G. "Our Berkshires: Spooks Are Still with Us." *Berkshire Eagle*, October 30, 1957.

Rushmore, Robert. "New Boston Chekhov: Inn of Indecision." *Berkshire Eagle*, August 17, 1976.

Saint Paul Globe. "Searles Has Wheels." July 10, 1899.

Sandusky Register. "Hush! Get the Sheriff!" July 22, 1911.

San Francisco Call. "Kellogg Terrace at Great Barrington." May 24, 1891.

San Francisco Chronicle. "A Fight for Millions: Remarkable Testimony of Mr. Searles." September 23, 1891.

———. "A Rich Woman Dead: Mrs. Hopkins-Searles' Life Ended." July 26, 1891.

Schweize, John. "Mysterious Mound Subject of Probe." *Berkshire Eagle*, July 16, 1970.

Sedgwick, Catharine M. "Magnetism Among the Shakers." *Sartain's Union Magazine* 4 (1849): 337–38.

Smith, Jenn. "Ghost Stories Hit Close to Home." *Berkshire Eagle*, October 31, 2006.

———. "On the Lookout for Cool Clean Water." *Berkshire Eagle*, June 30, 2005.

Springfield Sunday Union and Republican. "Burning of 'Haunted House' Recalls New Ashford Murder." December 28, 1930.

Standard Union. "October Mountain for Sale." August 8, 1920.

St. Louis Post-Dispatch. "The Hopkins Will." September 25, 1891.

Taylor, Holly A. "Bypass Survey Unearths Prehistoric Indian Sites." *Berkshire Eagle*, December 10, 1986.

Tichenor, Mary-Jane. "Fund-Raising Effort Mounted to Preserve Tyringham Ruin." *Berkshire Eagle*, June 19, 1999.

Trabold, Randy. "Rebuilding Fort Massachusetts." *North Adams Transcript*, August 16, 1969.

USA Today. "Haunting Music." July 30, 1992.

Wade, Lois Sharp. "Letter to the Editor: Give Up the Ghost on Highwood Haunting." *Berkshire Eagle*, August 7, 1992.

Walsh, Susan Besaw. "Potential Prison Site in Lenox Is Former Elegant Estate, Seminary." *Berkshire Eagle*, January 25, 1977.

Weil, Richard K. "Shadowbrook: The Demise of an Institution." *Berkshire Eagle*, July 30, 1970.

Wichita Daily Eagle. "Abandons Home to the Hoodoos." May 24, 1903.

Wilkes-Barre Leader. "Mrs. Searles and Great Barrington." August 20, 1891.

Williams, C.H. "In Behalf of Local History: An Appeal to Help Preserve the Local History of Northern Berkshire." *North Adams Transcript*, September 7, 1895.

Web Articles

All Things Medieval. "Searles Castle in Great Barrington Massachusetts." Castles. www.medievalcastles.stormthecastle.com.

American Centuries. "Fort Massachusetts, North Adams, Mass." www.americancenturies.mass.edu.

American National Biography. "Shaw, Robert Gould (1837–1863), Soldier: American National Biography." www.anb.org.

Asgari, Jeremy, et al. "Bash Bish Falls." Hike the Hudson Valley. www.hikethehudsonvalley.com.

———. "Composer Tracking 'Ghost' Who Apparently Likes Music." *Deseret News.* www.deseret.com.

———. "John Williams Composition About Ghost Making World Premiere." *Billboard.* www.billboard.com.

Atlas Obscura. "Bash Bish Falls." www.atlasobscura.com.

———. "Becket Land Trust Historic Quarry and Forest." www.atlasobscura.com.

———. "Mount Greylock." www.atlasobscura.com.

Backpackerverse. "10 Most Haunted Hikes in New England." www.backpackerverse.com.

Barlow, Rich. "An Inn with Berkshires History, Elegance." Boston.com. www.archive.boston.com.

Berkshire Eagle. "The Shaws at Lenox's Ventfort Hall." www.berkshireeagle.com.

Berkshire Hiking. "Tory's Cave." www.berkshirehiking.com.

Berkshires Online Guide to Events, News and Berkshire County Community Information. "North Adams Historical Society." www.iberkshires.com.

Berkshire Theatre Group. "History of The Colonial Theatre." www.
berkshiretheatregroup.org.
————. "New Beginnings for the Thaddeus Clapp House." www.
berkshiretheatregroup.org.
Brosky, Kerriann Flanagan. "A Winter Retreat in the Haunted Berkshires."
Patch. www.patch.com.
Cappa, Paula. "Ghosts on Mt. Greylock." www.paulacappa.wordpress.
com.
Cassidy, Benjamin. "Is Hancock Shaker Village Haunted?" *Berkshire Eagle*.
www.berkshireeagle.com.
Cinema Treasures. "Colonial Theatre." www.cinematreasures.org.
Commission Fears Fate of Fort Massachusetts." www.iberkshires.com.
CorpTrav. "13 Haunted Hotels to Avoid (Or Visit) On Your Next Business
Trip." www.corptrav.com.
Demartinis, Michael. "Fort Massachusetts." Historic North Adams, www.
historicnorthadams.com.
DeviantArt. "Vintage New England—The Shadow Over Mehkeenac by
Yesterdays-Paper on DeviantArt." www.deviantart.com.
Diana. "Bucksteep Manor." www.suburbhunting.blogspot.com.
Diaries, Ghost, et al. "Ghost Trains: A Haunting Look Behind the Legends."
Occult Museum. www.theoccultmuseum.com.
Dobrowolski, Tony. "Lenox Inn to Get $2.2M Upgrade under New Owner."
Berkshire Eagle. www.berkshireeagle.com.
————. "Mills: The Strength of Early Industry." *Berkshire Eagle*. www.
berkshireeagle.com.
————. "NYC-Based Nonprofit Buys Bucksteep Manor." *Berkshire Eagle*.
www.berkshireeagle.com.
Drew, Bernard A. "Haunted Chimney of New Ashford." *Berkshire Eagle*.
www.berkshireeagle.com.
Dupont Castle. "Searles Castle." www.dupontcastle.com.
Durwin, Joe. "A New Kind of Tourism Is Coming." www.pittsfield.com.
————. "Bizarre Berkshires: Tales Spooky and Otherwise." www.iberkshires.
com.
————. "The Decline of Loyalist Opposition in the Berkshires." www.
iberkshires.com.
————. "Haunted Travel: Where to Sleep with Ghosts in the Berkshires."
www.iberkshires.com.
————. "Pontoosuc's Lost Lovers Legend Is Classic Local Lore." www.
iberkshires.com.

————. "Tragedy Stained New Ashford's Haunted Homestead." www.iberkshires.com.

Edelman, Emily. "Bits and Bytes: 'A History of Searles Castle'; Downtown Pittsfield Trick or Treat; 'The Perfect Pitch'; 'Interreligious Illiteracy'; 'Stone Pears' Book Launch.'" *Berkshire Edge*. www.theberkshireedge.com.

Edwards, David Noel. "Leonard Bernstein and the Haunting of Highwood Manor House." *Berkshire Edge*. www.theberkshireedge.com.

EJourna. "Dead and Breakfasts—Great Places to Sleep with a Ghost." www.ejourna.com.

Ellis, Will. "Old Coot." AbandonedNYC. www.abandonednyc.com.

Erwin, Katharine. "4 Stunningly Haunted Waterfalls to Visit in the US." Adventure Sports Network. www.adventuresportsnetwork.com.

Explore North Adams. "Houghton Mansion." www.explorenorthadams.com.

Fanto, Clarence. "Longtime Families, Celebrities, Nature Prominent Here." *Berkshire Eagle*. www.berkshireeagle.com.

————. "Restoration Effort Aims to Give New Life to Seven Hills Ahead of Tourism Season." *Berkshire Eagle*. www.berkshireeagle.com.

Flammer, Joseph, and Diane Hill. "The Ghost of Room 301." Red Lion Inn. www.paranormaladventurers.com.

Fleming, Colin. "5 Haunted Hikes in New England: Do You Dare?" *Boston Globe*. www.bostonglobe.com.

Flint, Andrew. "Potter's Fields: Who do Those Unmarked Graves Belong To?" *Berkshire Eagle*. www.berkshireeagle.com.

Flynn, Patricia. "Ghost of Greylock." A Trish Out of Water. www.atrishoutofwater.com.

Fyden, Anthony. "The Five Most HAUNTED Places in the Berkshire Hills." www.iberkshires.com.

Gentile, Derek. "The Beauty and Sometimes Danger of Bash Bish Falls, Where Man's Body Still Lies." *Berkshire Eagle*. www.berkshireeagle.com.

————. "New Signs of 4,000-Year-Old Life at Kampoosa Bog." *Berkshire Eagle*. www.berkshireeagle.com.

————. "270th Anniversary of Fort Massachusetts Siege Commemorated." *Berkshire Eagle*. www.berkshireeagle.com.

Ghosts of America. "Becket, Massachusetts Ghost Sightings." www.ghostsofamerica.com.

Gonzalez, Lindsey. "Eight Real Haunted Houses in Massachusetts." *Boston Magazine*. www.bostonmagazine.com.

Gorlick, Adam. "For Sale: Old Massachusetts Castle; Dungeon Included." *Seattle Times*. www.seattletimes.com.

Haunted Journeys. "Becket Land Trust and Historic." www.hauntedjourneys. com.

Haunted Places. "Thaddeus Clapp House." www.hauntedplaces.org.

———. "Ventfort Hall." www.hauntedplaces.org.

Haunted Places to Go. "Paranormal Activity at the Houghton Mansion." www.haunted-places-to-go.com.

Haunted Rooms America. "The Houghton Mansion Ghosts, North Adams, MA." www.hauntedrooms.com.

———. "10 Most Haunted Hotels in America: What Is America's Most Haunted Hotel?" www.hauntedrooms.com.

Hidden Hills of Western Massachusetts. "Knox Trail Inn." www.hidden-hills.com.

History Hangout. "5 Haunted Bed and Breakfast Inns of Massachusetts." www.historyhangout.blogspot.com.

Hobomock, Evil Spirit of Wampanoag Legend (Chepi, Chipi, Hobomok). "Native American Legends: Hobomock (Chepi)." www.native-languages.org.

Hotel. "2017's Top 25 Most Haunted Historic Hotels from Historic Hotels of America." www.hotel-online.com.

Huberdeau, Jennifer. "Berkshire Haunts Host Ghost Tours for the Brave." *Berkshire Eagle*. www.berkshireeagle.com.

———. "Cemetery Tours: Uncovering a City's Past from the Ground Up." *Berkshire Eagle*. www.berkshireeagle.com.

———. "The Cottager: Highwood Manor: Where Hawthorne Dreamed up Tanglewood Tales." *Berkshire Eagle*. www.berkshireeagle.com.

———. "The Cottager: Searles Castle: A Mysterious Castle with a Mysterious Past." *Berkshire Eagle*. www.berkshireeagle.com.

———. "The Cottager: Seranak: A Perfect View of the Berkshires and Serge Koussevitzky's Private Life." *Berkshire Eagle*. www.berkshireeagle.com.

———. "The Cottager: Shadow Brook: A Cursed Cottage, or Just Unlucky?" *Berkshire Eagle*. www.berkshireeagle.com.

———. "The Cottager: Tanglewood: When Parties, Picnics on the Lawn Were Private." *Berkshire Eagle*. www.berkshireeagle.com.

———. "The Cottager: Ventfort Hall: From Shambles to Gilded Age Museum." *Brattleboro Reformer*. www.reformer.com.

IBerkshires.com. "North Adams Historical Society Observing Siege of Fort Massachusetts." www.iberkshires.com.

———. "Tracing the Mohicans in Berkshire County, Beginning in Stockbridge." www.iberkshires.com.

Jones, Trevor. "Historic Thaddeus Clapp House to Be Auctioned Off." *Berkshire Eagle*. www.berkshireeagle.com.

JWFAN, "'Highwood's Ghost,' New Williams Concert Work Premieres at Tanglewood (Audio)." www.jwfan.com.

Kolben, Deborah. "Castle Sale Seen Altering Berkshires Landscape." *New York Sun*, www.nysun.com.

Kreidler, Marc. "Ghosts at a Shaker Village." *Skeptical Inquirer*. www.skepticalinquirer.org.

Kripalu. "About Shadowbrook." www.kripalu.org.

Lamkin, Virginia. "Mt. Greylock's Old Coot." Seeks Ghosts. www.seeksghosts.blogspot.com.

———. "Pittsfield's Ghost Train." Seeks Ghosts. www.seeksghosts.blogspot.com.

Lamm, Everett. "The Ghosts of Searles Castle and the Whiting House." www.iberkshires.com.

Lenox Outing Club. "Tory Cave." www.lenoxoutingclub.weebly.com.

Leskovitz, Frank J. "The Lost Lovers of Pontoosuc Lake." Science Leads the Way. www.gombessa.tripod.com.

Leveille, Gary. "Knox Trail Revisited." *Berkshire Eagle*. www.berkshireeagle.com.

Levulis, Jim. "The Legends and Lore of Pittsfield." WAMC. www.wamc.org.

Lhowe, Mary. "Haunted Places of Massachusetts can Also be Cozy, Historic Inns and Restaurants, Too!" blog.visitnewengland.com.

Lineup, The. "America's Most Haunted Hiking Trails." America's Most Haunted. www.americas-most-haunted.com.

MacSweeney, Tim. "Monument Mountain and Other Indigenous Sacred Sites Condensed from Luci Lavin." www.wakinguponturtleisland.blogspot.com.

Marino, Paul. "Fort Massachusetts." www.paulwmarino.org.

Mass Mysteries. "October Mountain." www.massmysteries.blogspot.com.

Mathisen, David. "Sacred Stone Sites and Points of Connection with the Infinite Realm." Star Myths of the World. www.starmythworld.com.

Maynely Marketing Press Release. "Great Places to Sleep with a Ghost." www.maynelymarketing.com.

Merwin, Laura. "'Ghost Hunters' Investigate the Haunted, Historic Houghton Mansion in North Adams." Masslive. www.masslive.com.

———. "Photo Tour: Investigate the Haunted, Historic Houghton Mansion in North Adams, Mass." Masslive. www.masslive.com.

Mishkin, Shaina. "Six MORE Haunted Places in Western Massachusetts." Masslive. www.masslive.com.

NENI Web Team. "Ghost on the Thunderbolt." *UpCountry Magazine*. www.upcountryonline.wordpress.com.

New England Ghost Project. "Houghton Mansion." www.neghostproject.com.

New England Historical Society. "The Many Mansions of Edward Searles." www.newenglandhistoricalsociety.com.

Northeast Sporting. "October Mountain Whitney Estate." www.northeastsporting.com.

NPR. "The Sedgwicks: A History of 'Madness.'" www.npr.org.

O'Brien, Dr. Frank Waabu. "Spirit Names and Religious Vocabulary." Chapter 10: Spirit Names and Religious Vocabulary, www.bigorrin.org.

Oldest.org. "7 Oldest Bars That Ever Existed in America." www.oldest.org.

Omeka RSS. "Monument to the Stockbridge Indians." www.alplm-cdi.com.

Only in Your State. "This Delicious Restaurant in Massachusetts on A Rural Country Road Is A Hidden Culinary Gem." www.onlyinyourstate.com.

Owens, Carole. "Connections: Life and Loves in the Gilded Age." *Berkshire Edge*. www.theberkshireedge.com.

———. "Connections: Race Relations—Then and Now. How Indian Town Became Stockbridge." *Berkshire Edge*. www.theberkshireedge.com.

———. "Connections: Welcome Back Home, Mrs. Whistler." *Berkshire Edge*. www.theberkshireedge.com.

———. "Connections: When Meeting a Ghost, Mind Your Manners." *Berkshire Edge*. www.theberkshireedge.com.

Paranormal U.S. "Secrets of October Mountain." www.paranormalunitedstates.com.

Phelps, Brian. "Notable Phelps Family Members." www.phelpsfamilyhistory.com.

PineHawk. "Nikommo." www.pinehawk.abschools.org.

Pittsfield Massachusetts. "Thaddeus Clapp House." www.ihsadvantage.com.

Prosise, Kim. "The Most Insane Abandoned Places in Massachusetts." Thrillist. www.thrillist.com.

Redington, Pete. "Living Legends of the Dead." *Valley Advocate*. www.valleyadvocate.com.

Reily, Emily. "The Creepiest Haunted Places in Massachusetts." Thrillist. www.thrillist.com.

Revolvy. "Sedgwick Pie on Revolvy.com." www.revolvy.com.

Rivera, Erica. "5 Haunted Hotels to Visit This Halloween." Mandatory. www.mandatory.com.

Roadtrippers. "Becket Land Trust Historic Quarry." www.maps.roadtrippers.com.

Sakata, John. "Otis Man Calling Attention to Historic Revolutionary War Trail." *Berkshire Eagle*. www.berkshireeagle.com.

Scorzafava, Lauren. "The New Boston Inn: Lodging, Food, and Spirits?" Stella Cadente. www.stellacadenteblog.com.

Seaman, Donna. "Prominence, Privilege and Tragedy Mark the Sedgwick Family." *Chicago Tribune*. www.chicagotribune.com.

Seven, John. "Now Streaming…'New England Legends.'" *Berkshire Eagle*. www.berkshireeagle.com.

Shaffer, Bob. "How Western Massachusetts' Mount Greylock Became Inspiration for Literary Legends." ARTery. www.wbur.org.

Shanks, Adam. "Price Chopper Gives Fort Massachusetts Parcel to North Adams." *Berkshire Eagle*. www.berkshireeagle.com.

Shulman, Jim. "Jim Shulman: Baby Boomer Memories: North Street's Famous Diner." *Berkshire Eagle*. www.berkshireeagle.com.

Smith, Jenn. "Plaque Denotes Melville Trail in Pittsfield." *Berkshire Eagle*. www.berkshireeagle.com.

Sophia. "The Story Behind This Haunted Mansion in Massachusetts Is Truly Creepy." Only in Your State. www.onlyinyourstate.com.

———. "These 9 Haunted Hotels in Massachusetts Will Make Your Stay a Nightmare." Only in Your State. www.onlyinyourstate.com.

Travel Channel. "La Purisma Mission Haunted History." www.travelchannel.com.

Unexplained Mysteries Discussion Forums. "Phantom Train." www.unexplained-mysteries.com.

Urquhart, Rachel. "Driving New England Shaker Settlements." *Travel + Leisure*. www.travelandleisure.com.

Walsh, Lara. "25 Hotels You Can Stay in across the U.S. that Are Believed to Be Haunted." Insider. www.insider.com.

Webster, Rebecca. "Ghosthunters Head to Ventfort Hall to Investigate Paranormal Activity." *Berkshire Eagle*. www.berkshireeagle.com.

Westernmassparanormal. "Wizard's Glen—Haunted or Just Eerie?" www.westernmassparanormal.org.

Whatwhenhow RSS. "Houghton Mansion, North Adams, Massachusetts (Haunted Place)." www.what-when-how.com.

Williams College. "Ilvermorny on Greylock." www.williams.edu.

Writerjax. "Peeking into the Shadows at Ventfort Hall." www.writerjax.net.

Television and Video

Belanger, Jeff. *Connecting Point*. "New England Legends: Return to October Mountain." Aired on WGBY, December 15, 2014. www.youtube.com.

———. *Connecting Point*. "New England Legends: Ventfort Hall." Aired on WGBY, April 21, 2014. www.youtube.com.

———. "On the Search for the Old Coot of Bellows Pipe Trail—Mt. Greylock, Massachusetts." August 22, 2016. www.youtube.com.

———. *30 Odd Minutes*. "The Haunted Houghton Mansion." February 5, 2012. www.youtube.com.

Belanger, Jeff, and Ray Auger. "The Old Coot of Bellow Pipe Trail." *New England Legends Podcast*. Aired January 31, 2019. www.youtube.com.

Chicopee Paranormal. "Ghost Hunt at Ventfort Hall, Part 1." April 6, 2010. www.youtube.com

———. "Ghost Hunt, Haunting Ventfort Hall." September 15, 2010. www.youtube.com.

———. "Paranormal Activity at Ventfort Hall." May 9, 2011. www.youtube.com.

———. "Paranormal Investigation, July 3, 2010." May 9, 2011. www.youtube.com.

Cool Bike Rides. "New Boston Inn." August 15, 2009. www.youtube.com.

Moreau, Stephen, and Charles Reis. "Creepy Places of New England: The Becket Quarry." April 20, 2014. www.youtube.com.

Syfy. *Ghost Hunters*. Season 10, episode 9, "Houghton Hears a Who." Aired October 21, 2015.

———. *Ghost Hunters*. Season 1, episode 9, "New Boston Inn." Aired December 8, 2004.

———. *Ghost Hunters*. Season 3, episode 4, "Whispers and Voices." Aired November 1, 2006.

Things That Go Bump in the Night: Tales of Haunted New England. "The Old Coot on Mount Greylock." Aired on WGBY, 2009. www.youtube.com.

Websites

All Trails. www.alltrails.com.

Becket Land Trust. www.becketlandtrust.org.

Berkshire Historical Society. www.berkshirehistory.org.

Berkshiregirlonline. www.berkshiregirlonline.com.

Boston Symphony Orchestra. www.bso.org.
Elizabeth Freeman Mumbet. www.elizabethfreeman.mumbet.com.
Find a Grave. www.findagrave.com.
Ghost Quest. www.ghostquest.net.
Ghost Village. www.ghostvillage.com.
Great Barrington Historical Society and Museum. www.gbhistory.org.
Hancock Shaker Village. www.hancockshakervillage.org.
Haunted Journeys. www.hauntedjourneys.com.
Haunted Places. www.hauntedplaces.org.
Knox Trail Inn. www.knoxtrailinn.com.
Legend of the Lake Facebook Page.
Lenox History. www.lenoxhistory.org.
Massachusetts Haunted Houses. www.mahauntedhouses.com.
Massachusetts Historical Society. www.masshist.org.
Mass.gov. www.mass.gov.
Mass Moments. www.massmoments.org.
Mass ParaCon. www.massparacon.com.
Mount. www.edithwharton.org.
National Park Service. www.nps.gov.
New Boston Inn. www.newbostoninn.com.
New England Historical Society. www.newenglandhistoricalsociety.com.
Newspapers.com. www.newspapers.com.
Norman Rockwell Museum. www.nrm.org.
Official Western Massachusetts Paranormal Talk Forum. www.
    wmassparanormalforum.forumotion.com.
Red Lion Inn. www.redlioninn.com.
Sedwick.org. www.sedgwick.org.
Seven Hills Inn. www.sevenhillsinn.com.
Shadowlands. www.theshadowlands.net.
Stockbridge Bowl Association. www.thesba.org.
Stockbridge-Munsee Community. www.mohican.com.
These Mysterious Hills by Joe Durwin. www.mysterious-hills.blogspot.com.
Town of Otis. www.townofotisma.com.
Town of Sandisfield. www.sandisfieldma.gov.
TripAdvisor. www.tripadvisor.com.
Trustees of Reservations. www.thetrustees.org.
USHistory.org. www.ushistory.org.
Ventfort Hall. www.gildedage.org.
Whistler's Inn. www.whistlersinnberkshires.com.

Other Resources

Barrington Historic District Commission
Bernstein Centennial Celebration at Tanglewood Program
Hillsdale Public Library
Historic Great Barrington Walking Tour Brochure, by the Great Barrington
    Historical Society and The Great
Massachusetts Cultural Resource Information System
Massachusetts Historical Commission
Roeliff Jansen Historical Society
Taconic State Park Commission

INDEX

ABOUT THE AUTHOR

Robert Oakes is a writer, teacher, singer and songwriter from the Berkshires in Western Massachusetts. He has written for AAA, Canyon Ranch and a number of other publications and organizations, and he performs as part of the Berkshire-based folk music duo Oakes and Smith. Since 2010, Robert has led the ghost tours at the Mount in Lenox and has represented the museum and its ghosts on SyFy's *Ghost Hunters*, Jeff Belanger's *New England Legends* series on PBS and *The Apple Seed*, which is hosted by Sam Payne on BYUradio. Robert is currently pursuing his master's degree in English at the Middlebury Bread Loaf School of English in Middlebury, Vermont.